Where the He

Where the Heart Is

A writer in Provence

Marita van der Vyver

Translated by Annelize Visser

DOUBLE
STOREY
a juta company

To our guests

Published 2006 in English in southern Africa
by Double Storey Books,
a division of Juta & Co. Ltd,
Mercury Crescent, Wetton, Cape Town

First published in Afrikaans in 2004 as
Die Hart van ons Huis by Tafelberg Publishers

ISBN-10: 1 77013 035 7
ISBN-13: 978 1 77013 035 7

Copyediting by Sandy Shepherd
Page layout by Claudine Willatt-Bate
Cover design by Michiel Botha
Printing by Paarl Print, Paarl

Contents

1 We live in Church Street

Dear reader, let me introduce myself:

There are really several ways in which I could do this. If I wanted to create the illusion of exoticism, I could say that I was an Afrikaans writer living in a medieval village in the south of France. If I wanted to make a romantic impression, I could say that I lived in a Provençal stone house with lilac shutters, pink roses and lavender outside the kitchen window, and an enormous plane tree beside the gate. But if I were honest I would have to say that I am a tired housewife with a large family who lives in Church Street.

'That you've had to travel so far', my friend Michiel observes ruefully, 'just to end up in Church Street.'

That's probably what friends are for. To keep you in your place. And these days my place is in Church Street.

It may sound more exotic in French – *Rue de l'église* – but it remains a street with a church in a country village. Every country town, in France as in South Africa, has a Church Street. Fortunately, no French town also has a Voortrekker Street.

There are six of us in the house made of stone: my French husband Alain, me, and four children between the ages of three and seventeen. His, mine and ours. His two sons, Thomas and Hugo, don't live here all 365 days of the year. But if you add together all the weekends, the four short school holidays and the more than two months of the long summer holiday, they're here about half the time. My son Daniel finishes primary school in this village this year and will soon start *collège* (secondary school) in a bigger town. And our daughter Mia joined the baby class of the little local school last year.

It is said that there's an invisible line that runs somewhere through the middle of Europe. People who live above the line are large and blond and cook with butter. Those who live below the line are small and dark and cook with olive oil. We live in the olive-oil half of Europe – and we do cook everything with olive oil, except *frites* – but we don't look like olive-oil people.

Eleven-year-old Daniel and I are big and blond. At the moment Mia is still small and blonde but she's already taller than most of her classmates. Alain and Thomas have dark hair but neither of them is exactly small. They don't look as if they really belong here either. Thomas the Teenager has the longest hair in the village, which includes both men's and women's hair. His thick ponytail hangs way below his shoulder blades. Hugo, the same age as Daniel, is probably the closest our family will ever get to the Mediterranean look. Small, with dark hair and dark eyes, but far too pale to be considered an indigenous species.

That's us. But that's not all. In the summer our number increases on a daily basis. Provence in the summer is like Stilbaai in December: great fun for holidaymakers, less fun for permanent residents. Last summer we had sleepover guests every night for three months, sometimes five or six at a time. Along with the six of us, the teenaged Nephew from the North who spends every summer here, and Daniel's friends who hang around the Playstation in his bedroom like pot plants, this means large-scale meals every day – as in food for a church bazaar, meals for at least fifteen people at a time. No, make that twenty, because the three boys, the Nephew and the friends each eat like three normal people. They can't help it, they're at that age.

And then of course there's Mia's invisible double who goes by the name of Heloïse and draws on walls, messes with water and fiddles with the TV. In short, if mischief has been made, Heloïse gets the blame. Thank goodness Heloïse eats only invisible food. I mention her here just to avoid confusion later.

Fortunately, Alain likes to cook. Fortunately, he's the kind of cook who can conjure up a pot of soup for twenty people with just three onions and a carrot. I've learned to like cooking (what else could I do?), but I hate everything that goes with it: the shopping before, the cleaning up after, the dishes, the dishes, the dishes.

That's us. It's not as bad as it sounds. Pleased to meet you.

The church across the road from our house looks completely different from the Calvinist churches with their skinny white spires in the country towns of my childhood. And it's centuries older than any building in any town in the country of my birth. It's a Roman Catholic stone chapel that was built early in the twelfth century – as a newcomer from the Third World, I still marvel at that date – along with a Cistercian abbey next door.

The abbey was inhabited and guarded for a few centuries by a group of formidable nuns who weren't afraid of anything, not even bloodthirsty hordes. One of their legendary defence strategies was, for example, to release a swarm of bees from one of the towers at a horde of Protestant attackers. That is why residents of this village still have a rude nickname today, the local historian Jean-Pierre tells us over a glass of *pastis*, his moustache quivering with pleasure as his whispers the Provençal word. We don't understand the Provençal language (it is a language, the old folks tell us, not merely a regional dialect), but Jean-Pierre translates it for us into ordinary French – *pique-cul*. In ordinary English it means 'stung in the arse'.

Now I must introduce you to Jean-Pierre, because I cannot possibly paint the picture of our village without including his distinctive profile somewhere on the canvas. Jean-Pierre isn't really a historian. No one knows what Jean-Pierre really does to stay alive. In summer he sometimes helps the farmers pick fruit, in autumn he lends a hand with the grape harvest, in winter he potters around the tourist houses, laying roof tiles or floor tiles, acting the plumber or electrician, whatever is expected of him. But mostly he sits behind a glass of *pastis* in the local bar.

Every time I pop in for a quick coffee or to buy ice cream for the children, from early in the morning till late at night, I find Jean-Pierre there. Like a king on a throne, that's how comfortable he looks on his high bar stool, his black-olive eyes glittering in his bronzed face, his grey moustache always perfectly groomed and his grey-black hair combed back neatly. In his younger days he was apparently quite a Casanova. These days his stomach is probably larger than his libido or his vanity, but he still can't help kissing women of all ages on the hand and disarming them with flattery. The power of habit, that's all.

And because he's a proud *pique-cul* he considers himself an expert on everything to do with the life of any *pique-cul*. The history of the village, the weather of the region, the vineyards and the olives, the best wines, the most beautiful women, the funniest jokes. The other villagers tolerate his pedantry because most of them aren't authentic *pique-culs*. To earn this honorary title, you and your ancestors have to have lived here for generations, not in the next village three kilometres away. The next village is a different world.

When I asked our mayor one day if he was originally from this area (meaning the south of France, more or less), he sighed and reluctantly admitted that his mother's side of the family were 'newcomers'. They hadn't been here for two centuries. I thought he was joking in the deadpan way the French sometimes joke, and I started to smile. Until it dawned on me that he was serious.

That was the day I realised that my family and I would always be newcomers, *étrangers*, with the echo of the English word 'strangers'. Alain grew up in the north of France, which might as well be another country. And I grew up on a different continent. Another planet, you might say. This doesn't mean that we aren't treated with friendliness. Far from it. But we know our place.

Strangers we are and strangers we'll stay.

It's as if people in the French countryside have a collective memory that reaches back much further than even the oldest inhabitants' earliest memories. In this sunny region where tourism is the lifeblood of many small villages, foreigners are usually welcomed if not with open arms then at least with a pragmatic tolerance. What initially surprised me was that the arms opened more readily for Germans than for the British. This despite the fact that even the tiniest village has a monument with a shockingly long list of inhabitants who died in two bloody wars against the Germans in the last century.

'But the English were on your side!' I said to Jean-Pierre one day. 'The Germans were the enemy, weren't they?'

'*Bof*,' he said, 'we're now talking about the recent past. What is a war or two between neighbours? Remember, the English were the enemy for *centuries*. Look what they did to Jeanne d'Arc!'

Of course that's also why the French sided so enthusiastically with my Afrikaner ancestors during the Anglo-Boer War. It was simply a matter of principle. Any enemy of my enemy is my friend. When President Paul Kruger had to flee to Europe he travelled by train from Marseille to Paris, and at each station he was met by a crowd of cheering supporters. No other South African president would ever receive such a hero's welcome here – until Nelson Mandela came onto the scene almost a century later.

It is some consolation that we're not the only strangers in the village. Behind us, in a beautifully restored old farmhouse, lives a couple from Marseille. Marseille is barely an hour and a half away on the freeway – but it nevertheless belongs to a different universe, where people speak with a different accent, have different habits, eat different food. At any rate that is how the real *pique-culs* see it.

To our left, in a dignified three-storey building with grey-blue shutters, a jovial American has come to retire with his elegant Parisian wife and an Airedale terrier with a bandanna around its neck. Bad timing. Soon after their arrival the official relationship between the USA and France reached a historic low. During George W Bush's official war in Iraq, I, like most of the people in the village, never mentioned the war in this neighbour's smiling presence. He may have an impudent president, as eighty percent of the French believe, but the French have sympathy for people who have to live under an impudent president. (The year before it was touch and go whether France had Jean-Marie le Pen as its far-right president. And the current president's nickname is *Supermenteur*. Super-liar.) Besides, the American has chosen to live here rather than in America, in this village rather than in any other town in the world, which to the true *pique-cul* is sufficient proof of his intelligence and good judgement.

His charming Parisian wife probably elicits more mixed feelings.

Paris is the centuries-old 'enemy' of the French countryside, perhaps even more so than England. A case in point: a while back, a South African friend started farming in the French *campagne* after more than a decade in Paris. And I mean literally farm, as in driving a tractor and tilling the soil. Lynn the Farmer soon realised that it was better to say she was from Cape Town than to say she came from Paris. It's best not to mention Paris at all.

Her Parisian husband unfortunately can't pretend to come from South Africa, so he follows a different strategy. When questioned about his origins, he names a village close by where they briefly rented a house while looking for the piece of land of their dreams. In the *campagne* anything is better than being *Parisien*. Even being American is apparently better than being a Parisian.

Back in Church Street, or just around the corner from Church Street, there is also a big-hearted Moroccan family. Eighteen-year-old Hakima, with the long silky hair and almond-shaped eyes of a young Scheherazade, is the hard-working daughter who sometimes comes to help out in our house when the stream of guests gets so thick that we can no longer keep our heads above water – dishwater, washing-machine water, bathwater, when a dozen people and everything they use have to be kept clean every day. As in that haunting hymn of my childhood, Hakima believes that she mustn't go, or rather come, with empty hands to meet us. She always brings an offering – a bag of fresh sheep's liver (one of her many relatives works at an abattoir) or a box of delicious tomatoes (another relative works at a vegetable market) or a pot of steaming couscous her mother has just made. We're supposed to help Hakima earn pocket money (she's saving up for a driver's licence, an expensive business in this country), but sometimes it seems more as if it's her family helping to keep our family alive.

These are our closest neighbours – from Marseille, America, Paris and Morocco. But in case you start wondering if *everyone* around Church Street comes from somewhere else, let me quickly add that we do have at least one example of genuine *pique-culs* nearby. To our right a crooked little woman and her aged husband, the latter already a little senile, have lived for half a century in a simple farmhouse with dark-green shutters that's been in the family for goodness knows how long.

Outside this house there are no flowers or pot plants or any other useless decoration. Just a former chicken pen that's been refitted as a kind of store room, a washing line, a white plastic table and two plastic chairs. Sometimes on a sunny afternoon the crooked little woman sits at the table chopping beans. That's the closest this family ever comes to a meal in the open air. Which leads me to suspect that to genuine *pique-culs* our family's summer meals under the plane tree might seem a strange habit. Many other people in the village also like to eat outside in summer – in gardens, on patios, on verandahs. But then of course many others in this village are also newcomers. They haven't been here for two centuries.

What fascinates me about this house is that the shutters on the

second floor stay closed day and night. We've never seen even a
sliver of light in the top part of the house. Initially we thought
that the two old people used only the ground floor, as people here
do when they no longer have the time or the strength or the
money to maintain a large house. In our own triple-storey house
the top floor stayed wrapped in darkness for about fifty years
until our extended family and many guests began to inhabit the
dark parts again. And in Lynn the Farmer's enormous house the
previous owner used to live in a single room while the rest of the
building gradually fell to ruin.

But then we discovered that the house with the green shutters
had other inhabitants. At least two of the elderly couple's middle-
aged children live with them. We sometimes hear them arguing.
(It's nothing – our family makes much more noise when we
argue.) We greet them outside on the street. And on some nights
there are up to four cars parked in the gravel yard outside the
house.

But where do they all sleep? Do some live like moles on the
darkened second floor? Is there a secret annexe from World War
Two hidden somewhere behind a cupboard?

Perhaps I read too many war stories when I was young. But to
me it remains one of the great riddles of Church Street.

Despite what you may think, life in Church Street is not necessarily quiet. We are the only family with young children, but the tiny
square outside the church has been colonised by the village youth
as an ideal terrain for daring tricks with skateboards and
Rollerblades. This means that we regularly have to dispense plasters, and more than once we've had to call the fire brigade. Not
because the children set fire to the church, thank heavens, but
because the fire engine also serves as ambulance. Any child who
is rushed to hospital in the red fire engine, with screaming sirens,
is the hero of the square for at least a week.

Fortunately, there are no irresponsible young people nearby
who play ear-splitting music. But in our own irresponsible house-

hold anything from Led Zeppelin and Frank Zappa to Schubert and Mahler is sometimes played at ear-splitting volume. Many instruments, too. Thomas plays the bass guitar in a teenage rock band and practises in the sitting room for hours on end. Daniel started playing the trumpet last year and this year is learning the saxophone. Hugo recently also took up the guitar, Alain plays the harmonica and Mia plays the African drum in Thomas's bedroom. And me? I try to write stories in the midst of all the noise.

I should probably also tell you about the original compositions with which Alain and three of his colleagues regularly regale the whole street. My husband earns his living as a pedagogue – he works with learning-disabled and problem teenagers – but in his free time he belongs to a quartet that composes French *chansons*. Their songs may not be quite as noisy as those of the Rolling Stones – and yes, to be completely honest they're not quite as famous as the Stones – but every time they rehearse here in our courtyard it is clear that they are four frustrated, middle-aged rockers. They call themselves Sesame. I call them the Geriatric Jivers, but not when they can hear me.

Our closest neighbours, the elderly couple behind the green shutters, assure us that they don't mind the noise because they're both quite deaf. The couple from Marseille are spared the worst noise because our house has no windows facing them. And the American-French combination behind the grey-blue shutters are further away, beyond the immediate impact of the sound waves from our courtyard.

It's probably just the dead nuns who collectively turn in their graves every time Sesame's blues echo against the stonewalls of their convent.

But on a weekday, when the children are at school and the grown-ups at work, it does sometimes become wonderfully quiet in the street. Then it's just me and the soothing whirr of my computer. Sometimes the mistral wind howls around the corners of the house. Sometimes the cicadas sing as if they're taking part in a talent contest. In winter a few snowflakes may swirl past the window. In autumn the leaves of the plane tree flutter endlessly downwards to form a rustling orange-brown carpet outside the door. Once a day, come sunshine and rain, I hear our post-woman's scooter outside the gate. No other traffic, no noise, no excuse not to write. Alas.

Then I'm reminded again of why I'm here. Not to perpetually wash dishes or stick plasters onto other people's children's knees or listen to my husband's noisy *chansons*, but to write stories. And then I do that.

Our house was once upon a time the village bakery, Madame Voisine tells us, and until a few decades ago the American's house was the local school. Madame Voisine lives around the corner, opposite the *lavoir*, a kind of stone bath beneath a roof where for centuries the village women did their washing by hand. The good old days, Madame Voisine sighs, *le bon vieux temps*. Madame Voisine's nostalgia for the good old days beside the *lavoir* is mainly due to her insatiable curiosity about her neighbours' doings. Back then you could listen to the juiciest stories while scrubbing your sheets along with the other women. These days you sit all alone in your house and watch the sheets go round and round in your washing machine. These days you have to make so much more effort to find out what's going on in other people's homes!

As you can gather, our street was once the social nucleus of the village: the bakery, the school and the church so conveniently close together – feeding the stomach, the mind and the soul all in one place, so to speak – with the communal laundry and gossip mill just a few steps away. These days, residents must indeed make a bit more effort. The current bakery is a block away, the school a block further still. And the church is hardly used any more except for weddings and funerals.

The social nucleus, too, has moved, to a piece of open land behind the abbey. Here, on the banks of the Herein River, *boules* is played every summer afternoon. This is where you now hear the gossip you would previously have heard outside the church or at the laundry. *Boules*, also known as *pétanque*, is the common denominator in the village, the great equaliser, the binding factor between the *pique-culs* and the newcomers, between rich and poor, young and old. Even between men and women, these days. Although it remains a predominantly male game, in our village there are always women who play along.

The only distinction made is that between serious players and everyone else. The serious ones gather at an official ground – three tidy lanes, stone benches for spectators in the shade of stately poplars, a wire fence to keep out the philistines. The philistines, in other words everyone else, play in the parking lot, in the park, in the square outside the church, wherever they can find a level piece of ground. It doesn't have to be all that level either. The philistines play more for pleasure than for points. If the ground slopes a little to the right, or is so rocky that the iron balls veer off in unpredictable directions, that just makes the game more interesting. I know what I'm talking about. I'm one of the philistines.

Yes, I've also become a fan of *boules*. I'm a woman who's never had any patience with any sport before. But then, never before have I come across a sport that can be played with a glass of *pastis* in the hand.

Not that I'm much of a *pastis* drinker. The cloudy aniseed drink tastes too much like liquorice for my liking. No, rather give me the glorious light red wine from the Côtes du Rhône vineyards. Raspberry cooldrink is what I call it. Just the thing to quench your summer thirst. But I must admit I like the story of how *pétanque* originated.

Long, long ago it seems there was a more mobile Provençal ballgame called *la longue*. But on a historic summer's day in 1910, a player was too drunk to manage the three steps that the rules required you to take before you threw the ball. So he aimed his ball from a stationary position – and *voilà*, a new game was born. Born out of *pastis*, you might say.

That's our town. Feel free to close your eyes and imagine you are sitting on the verandah of the bar across from the *boules* ground. You can hear the *clink clink* of the iron balls and the babbling of the river. Somewhere from deep inside the bar you can probably also hear Jean-Pierre's voice. Haven't I told you he's always there? You can smell lavender and roses, ice cream and strong black coffee. And aniseed, of course. You raise the glass in your hand and take a careful sip of *pastis*. Just to see what it tastes like. *Santé*.

Well. That's the romantic version. The picture-postcard of life in Provence.

The rest of this book is all about what you won't find on a postcard.

2 Ten weddings and a funeral

The abbey opposite our house is still called *L'Abbaye*, but these days the triple-storey building with its large stained-glass window is used as a wine cellar. This is quite appropriate in this region around the Rhône River where wine has become a kind of religion. And believe me, a good bottle of Châteauneuf du Pape can indeed be a mystical experience.

But the church stays a church. Although it's no longer in use every Sunday, it is still a building where religious rituals are carried out. If you live opposite the church, these rituals inevitably influence the rhythm of your life. The hours of your day are measured by the bell in the stone tower. They say you get used to it, that after a while you don't hear it anymore, the way you stop hearing the trains when you live next to a railroad. That may be true, but I'm nevertheless grateful that our bell isn't one of those overzealous ones that sound every half-hour.

Our bell is polite enough to raise its voice just three times a day. And not in an arrogant way, more like a shy little cough. *Ting*, *ting*, *ting*. The first little cough comes at seven in the morning to make sure you're awake. Not quite loud enough to wake you if you're not. At twelve noon, another little cough sounds to wish you *bon appétit*. And at seven in the evening, a final little cough calls the children home from the street, to come and bath, set the table, do the homework. Truly a civilised bell.

When it comes to church rituals, however, the bell has a duty to perform. At Easter and Pentecost it calls urgently, pealing so that you can hear it throughout the village. If a couple are getting married, the bell shouts for joy. When someone is buried, the bell mourns. Slowly, solemnly, heartrendingly.

Fortunately, there are more weddings than funerals, especially in summer when brides come from far and wide, even from other countries, to marry in the romantic stone chapel and hold a dazzling reception in the former abbey next door. The dead don't come from far and wide, only from the immediate vicinity, and they die unscheduled throughout the year. But during summer I'd say that we have an exchange rate of around ten weddings for every funeral.

The weddings are both a pleasure and a pain for those of us who live under the church's wing. It's always exciting to watch the preparations, the stone staircase of the abbey being decorated with bows and flowers, the caterers and musicians delivering their equipment, all the bustle that reaches a climax with the noisy arrival of the wedding party. It's the custom here that every car in the wedding procession – and all passing cars, too – hoot loudly and persistently. Just so you'll know that a wedding procession is on the way when they're still in the next village.

But this noise is nothing compared to what you can expect late at night. Once the reception is in full swing, we lie in bed listening to booming techno-music, disco from the seventies, American pop from the eighties and nineties and – much worse – French pop from any era. Now and again we're surprised by a live music group that makes a more pleasant kind of noise. Last summer there was a jazz band hired by a wealthy British wedding party, which played the loveliest swing from the forties, with a hoarse singer who sounded exactly like Satchmo. We made our supper under the plane tree last until long past midnight and felt as if we had the most expensive seats at an excellent open-air concert. But something like that is a rare treat. Mostly you flee to your bedroom, close the windows and shutters, turn on the air-conditioning, hide your head under the pillows and hope for the mercy of sleep.

The worst trial of all comes at around four in the morning when the inebriated guests take their leave and loudly bid each other goodbye in the street just below our bedroom window.

Sometimes the festivities continue past sunrise. One morning recently I was standing in the kitchen, pouring coffee and yawning, when the previous night's bride appeared on the abbey steps like a hallucination. Still in her fairytale wedding gown, a wreath of flowers on her curled hair, her lips amazingly still painted pink, she showed no sign of exhaustion although she'd been dancing the entire night. While you could tell at a glance that *I* had just endured a night of erratic dreaming to the beat of a techno soundtrack.

And don't think it's all over once the last guest has finally left. Above all, don't think that you can go back to bed and catch up on the sleep you've lost. In a few hours the entire wedding party will be back to continue the celebration. The French call this tradition *le rebond*, 'the rebound', and according to my French husband it originated in the need to get rid of all the left-over food after the feast. In other words, you invite the previous night's wedding guests for lunch and at the same time they help you clean up the hall, wash the glasses and carry off the empty bottles. A practical bunch, the French, who know how to get dull things done in a delightful way.

But for our family in the stone house opposite the abbey, *le rebond* only means another restless Sunday after a restless Saturday night.

Now that I live here, I watch weddings the way other people watch sport: from the sidelines. I've been an official participant at just three French weddings – and one of those was my own rather modest one.

But where funerals are concerned, I've become a participant rather than a spectator. Not because I have a morbid interest in death, but because that's simply what's expected of you when you live in a small village. If anyone in the village whom you knew vaguely (and in a village like this you know everyone vaguely), or even a distant relative of someone you know vaguely, is buried, then you're there. Even Jean-Pierre temporarily abandons his throne in the bar to perform his duty. Weddings are exclusive occasions to which a limited number of guests are invited. Funerals are open to everyone. The more the merrier.

No, I don't suppose you can say that.

And yet I'm surprised time and again, especially at the funerals of older people, by how many of the guests don't look sad at all. They don't even go inside the church (granted, the church is usually packed anyway), but stay outside and talk during the service. Nothing about their appearance makes you suspect that they're funeral-goers. And I don't just mean the lack of sanctimonious sadness, I'm talking about the way they're dressed. Nowhere is there a sober black suit or a smart black dress in sight. Nowhere a tie or even a pair of high-heeled shoes. The men, farmers mostly, look as if they've come straight from the field to quickly bury old Roger or Rolande. In winter they wear muddy boots; in summer, work shoes covered in dust. The women usually remember to remove their aprons, but make no effort beyond that.

Madame Voisine, who of course never misses a funeral, has a lifelong aversion to black. She reminds me of Edith Piaf, such a little bird of a woman with a sharp beak for a nose, but unlike Piaf you'll never ever see her in a black dress. The furthest she'll go for the sake of the departed is perhaps a blouse with a dark-blue pattern. Frightfully demure compared to the brightly coloured patterns she usually wears. But even in her quietest outfit there is no risk that she'll blend into the crowd. Not with a head of hair like hers. For years, Madame Voisine's thin fuzz of hair has been dyed as orange as the inside of a ripe melon. Forget the Sparrow of Paris. Meet the Parrot of Provence.

At my first funeral here in the countryside I felt as if I'd turned up at a braai in my Sunday best. Not that my clothes were all that smart, I'd just traded my usual jeans and walking boots for a black skirt, black tights and flat black shoes. But it was in the middle of winter and I was the only woman under eighty braving the icy cold in a skirt. There were exactly four frock-wearers in the church – two ancient crones, the priest and me. And the priest was wearing several layers of clothing underneath his frock to keep him warm. After the church service, when the entire funeral procession braved the steep hill to the cemetery on foot in a swaying row behind the incense-swinging priest, I cursed my unsuitable black city shoes with every laboured, muddy step.

Back home I tried to warm my frozen toes in front of the fire and promised myself that for the next funeral I'd dress better. Or worse, as my grandmother would have said. Less proper, at any rate. Next time I'd keep my jeans and my hiking boots on.

But when the next funeral came, it was as if I heard my grandmother's voice somewhere: 'That simply wouldn't do, my dear. One must have respect for the dead, you know!' And respect, according to my grandmother, just doesn't lie in jeans and boots. At the last minute I ripped off my jeans and put on a more decent pair of pants. More decent shoes, too.

It's now many funerals later – and I'm still struggling with the casual dress code. Where I grew up, a funeral was a terribly black, terribly formal, terribly terrible business. Imagine my surprise when at a recent funeral I spotted the deceased's teenaged sister dressed in frayed jeans and tackies and on her head a knitted hat with a picture of a marijuana leaf. She's a lovely girl who certainly wasn't trying to provoke anyone. That's just the way teenagers look around here – whether they're going to the shop, to school or to church.

It's not just the informal clothes that make funerals here different from the ones I'm used to. Everything is different, from the custom of going to look at the body to the appearance of the hearse. Where I grew up you didn't look at dead people. Except when you saw them lying in the road after a car accident. But the dead people you knew, those you didn't look at. They were nailed into a coffin and dug deep into the ground as soon as possible. Or handed over to a crematorium and shoved into an oven. Where I grew up we didn't decorate the body like the ancient Egyptians, we didn't wrap the body in a cloth and feed it to the fish like the seafarers of old, we didn't watch the corpse being consumed by flames as Indians do and we certainly didn't get drunk beside it like those wild Irishmen. We Calvinists prefer to pretend that the body isn't there. The spirit is all that really matters.

Where I live now, there is no such vigorous denial of the bodily remains. Here the dead is a physical presence, an object to be exhibited so that the entire neighbourhood can say good-bye. I've seen more dead people up close in the few years I've lived here than in nearly four decades in South Africa.

And to my amazement it isn't a frightening thing. Granted, the first time I turned as pale as the corpse with shock but that was just because no one had warned me that there was a dead person in the living room. All I wanted to do was to write my name in the thick book that's always placed on a small table outside the house where someone has died. It's one of those things that are expected of you when you live here. A neighbour's elderly mother had died and when I asked an unknown relative where the neighbour was, meaning of course the living one, he thought I meant the dead one and pointed to the lounge. The moment I entered I realised that the room was as cold as a fridge and as silent as the grave. And there the dead neighbour lay flat on her back in front of the TV.

At least the TV was switched off.

I was equally shocked the first time I saw a hearse that didn't look like a hearse. Not even black. A four-wheel-drive vehicle, something between a Land Rover and a station wagon, in a dark shade of blue. Now that I've become an experienced funeral-goer I know that most village cemeteries lie at the top of the highest hill in the area. I don't know if it has something to do with respect for the dead, but around here the most breathtaking views are often reserved for them. As an experienced funeral-goer I also know that the winding paths that lead to these final lookout posts would be too much for any 'ordinary' hearse, particularly in winter when everything is covered in mud or snow. Now a four-wheel-drive makes perfect sense to me.

What still doesn't quite make sense, even after numerous funerals, is the odd appearance of the undertakers. All right, I suppose one has to be a little odd to want to become a funeral undertaker but I can't recall that the species ever caught my attention in South Africa. On the contrary. There they are usually the proverbial little grey men who melt into the curtains, as if they'd been trained to become invisible. Here in the French countryside they look like characters from *The Addams Family*.

On our local team there is, for example, a formidable woman with muscular arms, cropped hair, a dark-blue men's suit and a tie. (It took three funerals before I realised she was a woman.) One of her colleagues is a tattooed tough guy with the shoulders of a bull and the nose of a boxer. At first I speculated that they were chosen purely on account of their muscles, to ensure that they're able to carry even the heaviest coffin. But then I saw the third colleague. A skinny, middle-aged little man who looks as if he could barely manage the weight of the black-rimmed glasses on his nose, with false teeth that threaten to pop out every time he opens his mouth. I suppose muscles alone couldn't keep a funeral parlour in business. Perhaps he is the brain behind the undertaking. The fourth member of the group, apparently the leader, has grey hair, a paunch, and the poker face of a government official. He doesn't really do anything. He just stands there with hands folded and a prim frown. I suspect he was hired to lend the illusion of normality to his bizarre colleagues.

The liveliest show in town. That was the observation made by a South African friend who watched two funeral processions outside our house last year. Actually, there are just three shows in this village. Funerals, weddings and the *boules* played alongside the river. And believe me, I've seen enough of all three to agree with my friend. Sometimes a funeral is indeed the liveliest entertainment in a French country village.

3 Things you miss

'What can we bring you? What do you miss the most over there? Biltong? Mealie meal? Rooibos tea?'

Like the Three Wise Men the kindest guests always bring an offering from the Beloved Country. I've been asked so many times what I can't get my hands on here, which gift would make my heart leap with joy, that these days I constantly walk around with a little list in my head.

Of course I'm talking about things you can pack in a suitcase. What I miss most are people and places, family and friends, Table Mountain and Kogel Bay. Things even the guest with the best intentions cannot bring me. But it is nevertheless remarkable how a gift that's been lugged all the way from Africa can make a gloomy day seem less grey.

I'm talking above all about food and drink. Grape jam and green fig preserve. Chutney and dried sausage. Koeksisters and clingstone peaches. Yes of course you can buy a fantastic variety of fresh fruit at a Provençal morning market. But I've never found peaches that crunch under your teeth like those gigantic, bright-orange, syrupy-sweet peaches of the Boland.

So – all the typical and traditional South African treats. Everyone knows that's what one misses. What keeps surprising my guests is that these items are fairly low down on my list. Not that I'd spurn a strip of biltong, far from it, but in the French countryside there are so many other things I can't find. Things I'd never thought I'd miss because I was barely aware that I was using them. Things that were just always there.

But now I'm here and these things aren't, and suddenly they acquire a significance that they don't really deserve.

Food colouring, for example. Those cute little bottles of blue, red and yellow liquid with which you colour the icing for your child's birthday cake. French children apparently don't know such colourful cakes. French *mamans* probably consider such cakes a little vulgar. On little Alexandre's or Amélie's birthday, *maman* buys a cake at the *pâtisserie*, usually a cake that resembles a work of art, an elegant creation with glacé fruit or chocolate curls, something you want to frame and display on a wall. Nothing like the children's cakes I know.

The children's cakes I know look like toys. Trains and helicopters, pirates' chests and castles. Colourful and kitsch. The taste is completely unimportant. A dozen excited children will each take one bite and leave the rest in a messy heap on their paper plates. That's how it works where I come from.

So imagine how panic-stricken I was when Daniel celebrated his first French birthday and I couldn't find a little bottle of colouring anywhere at all. How do you have a children's birthday party without coloured icing? In the end I baked a chocolate cake in an elephant-shaped cake tin and covered the whole thing in chocolate spread. A brown elephant, I told Daniel. Nice African touch. The tin I'd fortunately brought from South Africa. In France cakes looks like cakes – or works of art – but certainly not like elephants.

By Daniel's next birthday I was prepared. In the grocery cupboard an entire collection of little colouring bottles waited like soldiers on a parade ground – thanks to a few guests who'd responded to my strange request. At least one of these guests probably cursed me during the rest of her European trip. A bottle of red colouring had shattered inside her suitcase. Her clothes, underwear, accessories and books had all been dyed interesting rosy shades from salmon to mulberry.

Speaking of red, red jelly is also unobtainable. So is any colour jelly, actually, but red jelly is what I need for the trifle I try to make every Christmas. I say try, because up until now I've not yet managed to produce a trifle that tastes remotely like my mother's traditional one.

Every family has its Christmas traditions. And for mine Christmas just isn't Christmas without a bowl of trifle that reminds you of an old-fashioned church bazaar. I mean my South African family of course. Here in France you eat oysters and truffles and for dessert a kind of ice-cream cake in the shape of a tree trunk. I don't mind the oysters and the truffles and all the other pleasures, not at all, but I put my foot down when it comes to the tree-trunk cake. Tradition is tradition.

Believe me, when you're living far from your native soil, tradition can suddenly become quite important.

But the first time I attempted my mother's traditional recipe in France, I discovered that the French didn't know what jelly was. Nor custard powder. The closest thing to good old English custard around here is an instant dessert that is sold in yoghurt containers. *Crème anglaise*, they call it. English cream. I suppose I could have tried to make the required custard by hand, the old-fashioned way, but I was too lazy and too cowardly, my courage already broken by my pathetic attempt to manufacture jelly.

Because I hadn't been able to find an instant dessert resembling jelly, I'd tried to devise it myself with boiling water and sheets of gelatine and far too much sugar and red food colouring. (Thanks again to the guests who brought the colouring. Had I known better I would have asked them to bring a few packets of jelly powder as well.) It was a complete disaster. In appearance, texture and taste. The colour had turned out more brown than red, the liquid wouldn't set and it tasted like cough syrup.

But I was so determined to have trifle on the table that I used this cough-syrup concoction in place of red jelly. And *crème anglaise* from yoghurt containers instead of good old custard, and a local sweet wine by the name of Rasteau (a village just on the other side of the hill) instead of South African sweet wine. A Boer makes a plan, I proudly announced to my family. But the plan doesn't always work, does it?, Daniel mumbled when he surveyed the business. Aside from me he was the only one who knew what trifle was supposed to look like. But even Alain and his French sons knew that it couldn't look like *this*. Cake crumbs and peach slices floating in cough syrup.

Everyone knows a Coke float, Daniel giggled, but this is the first time he's seen a cake float.

I usually have an adequate sense of humour, but that was a joke I failed to appreciate.

Another thing that's unavailable here is whole-wheat flour. Not to mention bran. Maybe the health shops in the big cities stock these things, but we live far away from any big city. And however fond I am of a fresh *baguette* or a buttery croissant, sometimes I miss a thick slice of whole-wheat bread. Or whole-wheat rusks.

Perhaps this is the taste I miss the most. A hunk of whole-wheat rusk dunked in coffee. Slowly sucking the coffee from the rusk.

In South Africa I simply popped into the nearest home industry shop once a week to top up my supply of rusks. I seldom left without a few other treats as well: fudge or koeksisters or coconut ice, ostensibly for Daniel and his friends. And a bunch of arum lilies or sunflowers for the house.

In France there's nothing that could remotely be compared to a home industry shop. Nowhere would find such an eclectic mix of cakes and flowers and knitted baby booties and crocheted toilet-roll covers. Only intimidating *pâtisseries* where breath-taking little chocolate creations are displayed behind shiny glass. Confectionery museums, that's what they make me think of. I can't imagine anything as inelegant as a whole-wheat rusk ever turning up in such a museum. As unimaginable as Tretchikoff's *Blue Girl* in the Louvre.

But what do you do when visions of rusks haunt your dreams at night? When you know that the next day (and the one after that) you're going to have to be satisfied with yet another croissant? They say necessity is the mother of invention. In my case, necessity was the mother of baking.

Yes, I conquered my lifelong fear of the oven. I started baking my own rusks. As with the trifle for the Christmas table, the first few attempts were tragic flops. As with the trifle, I had to substitute certain unobtainable ingredients with others. Instead of the whole-wheat flour I know, I use what the French call *farine complète*, an insipid beige version of ordinary white flour. Instead of a handful of bran I use whole-wheat cereal that I crush with my foot.

The foot-crushing I learnt from *Two Fat Ladies* on TV. You put the breakfast cereal or the biscuits or whatever in a plastic bag on the floor and you stamp your foot as if you're furious. Much more effective than crushing it with a rolling pin – and also an excellent way of getting rid of everyday frustration. As you can tell from my three-year-old daughter's theatrical foot-stamping.

Instead of buttermilk, which is apparently unknown in these parts, I use several containers of natural yoghurt.

Slowly but surely my rusks have been improving.

My mother's favourite recipe requires two teaspoons of baking powder, two teaspoons of bicarbonate of soda *and* two teaspoons of cream of tartar. Don't ask me why. The baking powder isn't a problem. The bicarbonate of soda I eventually found at the chemist, after an extensive search among the flour and other cake-related ingredients in several supermarkets. The cream of tartar remains the missing link in my rusk evolution. In the end I started using a different recipe.

Last week I took the best batch of rusks ever out of the oven. The ladies at the home industry shop would've been proud of me. But I feel a bit like I do when I'm praised for a book I've written.

I want to protest, I want to confess, I want to say that I didn't do it entirely on my own. Readers usually forget about the important role played by a writer's editor in a book's success. And this time one of this writer's editors played a deciding role in the success of her rusks.

Like any good guest, Louise Steyn, faithful editor of my youth novels, had asked what she could bring along when she visited this region a while ago. A packet of whole-wheat rusks, I'd pleaded, although by this time I knew that rusks made a rather impractical parcel in a tourist's suitcase. Usually it's just a heap of crumbs that arrives at the other end. But I was so desperate that I was prepared to eat crumbs.

And then Louise astonished me by travelling through Europe with an enormous Tupperware of rusks in her arms (in the aeroplane, I suspect, she cradled it in her lap the entire night), determined that this time I wouldn't eat crumbs.

I was still stammering my thanks when she completely floored me by producing a paper bag with 5 kg of whole-wheat flour from her suitcase. As any tourist knows, 5 kg is an enormous load when your entire luggage allowance is 20 kg. Just imagine everything she must have left behind for the sake of a sack of flour!

Thanks to this sacrifice, above and beyond any editor's duty, I can bake proper whole-wheat rusks for the next few months. I eat each batch slowly. I hide it from the children. It isn't nice, I know, but it has to be done. Daniel and Mia are formidable rusk eaters. Maybe it's hereditary. What baffles me is that even Hugo has developed an inexplicable craving for whole-wheat rusks. He was born in France, he eats only white bread and until recently he didn't even know that something like rusks existed. Now he rummages around the kitchen at night and the next morning I follow the trail of crumbs all the way to his bed. Now I'm beginning to wonder if the passion might not be contagious.

In the meanwhile I'm going to keep hiding my rusks. I don't think I'll soon find another guest who is willing to tour Europe carrying a massive bag of flour.

4   Paper equals panic

Render unto Caesar the things that are Caesar's, is what we were taught at school. But now school is a long way away, I live in another country and I've learnt a new law: paper is power.

Long ago I thought that paper was something delicate that could be crumpled, torn up or set alight. Now I know better. Paper is something mighty that should be copied, certified and signed, watched like gold or wielded like a weapon.

Paper is omnipresent and inescapable. Paper is king, Caesar and president. If you want to live in a different country, you have to learn to respect paper.

Maybe things are different in England or Australia or one of those Anglo-Saxon countries where nowadays computers are widely used to facilitate administrative matters. But in France state officials still seem to harbour grave suspicions about computers. Technology is used simply because it is there, but information isn't really regarded as information unless it is written on paper. Copied, certified and signed.

Every time I find myself at a *mairie* or *préfecture* – the French versions of municipal offices or provincial headquarters – I become depressed at the sight of all those shelves filled with files. Just imagine how many trees had to be felled to manufacture all that paper.

The other emotion that regularly overwhelms me in a *préfecture* is a little less worthy of me. It's a kind of blind envy of the Voortrekkers of days gone by who could embark on their Great Trek without papers. Anyone who tried to stop them along the way was summarily mowed down. It's not a tactic of which I approve, of course. But on more than one occasion in the past few years I've had to fight a primitive urge to threaten an unhelpful French bureaucrat with an old-fashioned muzzle-loader.

I don't want to haul an ox wagon across a mountain. I am genuinely grateful that I was able to load my earthly possessions onto a sturdy ship. But my life would've been so much easier if my modern Great Trek was a paperless saga.

It's not just foreigners who can be driven insane by the French obsession with papers. Every French child receives a *carnet de santé* at birth, a 96-page book in which every doctor's visit, inoculation, disease and injury of its first few years will be recorded in detail. After that the *carnet* is supposed to accompany the child throughout its entire school career. When I wanted to enrol my five-year-old son at the local school, the headmaster refused to admit him because he didn't have such a book. Who knew what horrible diseases he'd brought with him from Africa? I waved his official inoculation certificate about. So it was just a single sheet of cardboard, I protested, but it contained all the necessary details. What more could they want?

They wanted more. About 95 pages more. No French official will be satisfied with one page if he can get 96.

No, it's not just foreigners who struggle to keep head above paper, but it's worse if you're from another country. The French are used to it. I suspect that French babies are born with a piece of paper in their hands, a tiny certificate that grants them permission to leave the womb. If you were born elsewhere it can take a lifetime to get all these papers together. If you're an adult by the time you start this paper trail, you're like a lame marathon runner who starts the race an hour after all the other runners. You're never going to catch up. By the time you've got your hands on every possible piece of official paper, they'll have thought up a few new ones.

Sometimes you end up in situations so absurd that it would make Kafka gasp. With me it has happened a few times. Once it was on a sweltering summer's day in Valence, which was my administrative capital at the time. Soon afterwards it became Avignon, and now it is Valence once again, because I've moved house twice, just a few kilometres from my previous address in each case, but each time I ended up in a different administrative department and a different geographical region. Not that I blame the French for that. It was my own ignorance that made me decide to settle exactly on the border between several departments and regions. But I do blame the French for the abyss of red tape into which each of these moves plunged me.

Valence is a good four hours' drive, there and back, from the village where I first came to live. Every time I had to drive to Valence to hand in yet another obscure piece of paper, an entire day was therefore lost because once you've landed inside the *préfecture*'s enormous fortress you usually have to wait a few hours before it is finally your turn to talk to an official. Assuming that by this time the official hasn't disappeared to uphold that all-important French tradition known as the extended lunch.

And then you still have to reckon with the unpredictable hours kept by government offices. I kept Daniel out of school one day because he had to be identified as the child on the picture I had to hand in – and we ended up outside a dark, deserted building. I'd chosen the one day of the week on which the *préfecture* of Valence closed its doors. Which is not necessarily the same day on which the *préfecture* of Avignon – or the bank in the neighbouring village – closes its doors.

It's so much easier in a country where you know that from Monday to Friday, between nine and five, you work (or pretend that you're working), and on weekends you rest. Nothing is ever that simple here in the south of France. Our local supermarket is closed on Sunday afternoons and all day on Monday; the bar is open all day on Sunday but closed all day on Monday; the baker and the hairdresser close on Wednesday; my favourite café in the vicinity closes on Thursday. The post office is open every day (in theory anyway), but for barely two hours in the morning and less than two hours in the afternoon. The library is open only in the morning on some days and in the afternoon on others ...

It's a logistical nightmare. You have to consult a complicated timetable on the fridge every time you want to buy a loaf of bread.

These days I don't drive to a *préfecture* without first making sure that I'll find somebody home. I learnt my lesson the hard way. But in those early days I had quite a few lessons yet to learn. For example, that *Catch-22* wasn't just the title of an entertaining novel.

On this scorching hot day in Valence the woman at the *préfecture* refused to give me a temporary residence permit unless I had a social security number. So I walked over to the *Sécurité Sociale*, yet another enormous fortress a few blocks away, to get the required security number. But here a grumpy *monsieur* refused to give me a security number unless I had – wait for it – a temporary residence permit.

Catch-22.

Back to the *préfecture* to explain. Back to the *Sécurité Sociale* to plead. Back to the *préfecture* to explain, to plead and to threaten ...

I was seven months pregnant, heavy and sweaty with swollen feet, and on each slow journey between the two buildings the sun burnt a hole right through my scalp. After a few hours of this absurd form of torture I subsided onto the steps outside one of the two buildings and started to cry inconsolably. *By Grand Central Station I Sat Down and Wept*. For the first time I really understood what Elizabeth Smart meant when she chose this sad title for her novel. While outside a government building in Valence I sat down and wept.

Another day, another low. This time in Avignon, which had in the meantime become the seat of all my administrative resentment. One of those days in late winter when the mournful mistral sucks every last bit of the life-urge from your body.

Let me first explain about the mistral.

I promise I'll never complain about the Cape southeaster again. The Cape southeaster is a pleasant breeze compared to the Provençal mistral. Yes, it's true that the southeaster flings you against lampposts and in front of cars, but it lasts only a couple of days and, once you've survived the onslaught, the peninsula always looks more beautiful than before. The clean air above Table Mountain is enough to make you instantly forget the annoying wind. The Provençal mistral is stronger than the southeaster, colder than the southeaster and, above all, more persistent than the southeaster. The mistral blows for up to thirty days at a time. During my first spring here, there were exactly three windless days in the whole of April.

According to our local meteorologist Jean-Pierre, the fertile Rhône Valley acts as a kind of bellows for a wind that is born in the Alps – although its icy breath sometimes makes you suspect that it comes straight from Siberia – and then blasts open its way to the warm Mediterranean Sea. A simple explanation, therefore, but not the sort of thing you're likely to read in tourist brochures. If all those sun-starved crowds heard that their hard-earned Provençal holiday could be blown away before their eyes, day after day after day, they certainly wouldn't come here in such droves.

Be that as it may. It was on one such wind-ravaged day that we stood in Avignon in front of the desk of a clerk who had to issue a temporary travel permit to Daniel so that he'd be readmitted to the country at the end of a family visit to South Africa. No happy holiday lay ahead of us. My mother had died in South Africa in the same week my daughter was born in France. Now, about two months later, the baby was strong enough for us to embark on the long journey to go and bury my mother's ashes.

Well, in actual fact the baby had been strong enough a month earlier, but it had taken two months to obtain all the papers required for the journey – including a new passport for the new family member, a renewed French passport and an international driver's licence for Alain. Only Daniel's bit of paper still had to be arranged. Just a final formality. Or so we thought. After all we were armed with every possible official paper the child had ever received in his life, from his birth certificate to his school reports, you name it.

And then the woman behind the counter asked – with a face that said 'Here comes trouble' – if I could prove that I was the child's mother.

'But of course,' I said indignantly. 'Look, there is my name on his birth certificate!'

'*Non, non,*' she said. This certificate was in English. She needed one that had been translated into French.

'But it's only a question of a few names!' I objected. 'Our names are still our names, whether they're written in English or in French!'

'*Non, non,*' she said. Rules were rules. She couldn't issue the permit unless I supplied a translated birth certificate.

Well then, I'd quickly go and translate it on my computer, I said in an attempt to make peace (because we had to leave for Cape Town in a week), and hand it in the next day.

'*Non, non.*' Her face sagged like a *soufflé* that's been taken from the oven too soon. It had to be an official translation. By an official translator. Certified with an official stamp. And that wasn't all. (Here comes the really bad news, I knew right away.) This birth certificate wouldn't do, translated or not, because it wasn't the correct one.

What did she mean it wasn't the *correct* one? The child had been born only once! He'd been given only one certificate to mark the occasion!

No, she explained. This was an abridged version. She needed the full certificate, freshly issued by the relevant state department in the child's country of birth, less than three months before. At these words the prospect of our South African family visit disappeared like a ship on the horizon. No, not as calmly as that, more like a ship falling over the edge of a waterfall. I knew by now that any application for official documents from South Africa, via the South African embassy in Paris, meant a wait of two to three months. There wasn't any way that I could get my hands on a full certificate – let alone an official translation – in the week before we were supposed to fly to Cape Town.

And at that moment of unbearable tension the clerk decided to close her counter and go and enjoy her lunch.

Our forlorn little group – Alain, Daniel, Mia in her pushchair and me – didn't have lunch that day. We wandered through the wind-torn streets of Avignon trying to figure out how we would get to South Africa. Or rather, how we could ensure that Daniel would be able to return with us to France. Surely provision had to be made for special circumstances, I murmured half-hopefully. If I explained that it was about my mother's death? But Alain, who knows the French better because he is one of them, shook his head sadly. *Non, non.* Rules were rules.

In the end we phoned the South African embassy in Paris – who fortunately have shorter lunch hours than the French in Avignon – to ask if they could help. I know a few people who work there. Well, I haven't actually met them personally, but I've phoned them for help so many times that they feel like distant relations. And to be sure, the capable Ms Anker (one of my almost-relations) promised to have an affidavit drawn up, in French, to say that I was Daniel's mother. And to fax it directly to the office in Avignon. I just had to give her the fax number and the name of the head of the office.

With renewed courage we now waited for the clerk's return. We hoped that she'd enjoyed a pleasant lunch so that she would be in a more accommodating mood when she resumed her place behind the counter. And indeed she was looking less grim – there was even the hint of a smile at the corners of her mouth – when we stood in front of her once more. Incredible how the mood of a French citizen can be influenced by a plate of food.

But the smile disappeared the moment we asked to see the head of the office. *Non! Impossible!* Just for five minutes, we pleaded, just to explain about the sworn statement the South African embassy was going to send. *Impossible!* All right then, we sighed, rules were rules after all, but could she please give us the person's name and fax number? *Impossible*, the clerk said.

And suddenly I snapped. After nearly two years of silent suffering at the hands of the French bureaucracy, I'd reached breaking point. I stamped my foot on the floor like a naughty child and my face turned an unattractive red and I raised my voice. I refused to leave until I'd spoken to the office head. I would spend the night here if I had to! I would cling to the furniture if the police tried to drag me away!

Fortunately at this stage my French was still so bad that the terrified clerk didn't understand half my desperate threats. What she did understand was that she was dealing with a woman on the brink of insanity. She grabbed the telephone and muttered a few anxious words into the mouthpiece. See, I cried to Alain (who was rubbing my back as if I was a growling dog that needed to be pacified), sometimes you have to be rude to get your way! There you are, she's phoning the office head! He wasn't so sure, Alain mumbled, he thought she might be calling the security guard to come and remove me.

But she was indeed calling the office head. Who still refused to see us, but did give the clerk permission to reveal the highly secret telephone number to us. Alain immediately walked outside with his cell phone and, huddling against a window for protection from the vicious wind, dialled the number. He heard the phone ring right behind him, he heard a woman's voice answer the phone on the other side of the window, he heard the same voice in his ear. Could he see her for a few moments? he asked. No, she said, she was busy. Yes, he said, he could hear that she was busy – busy talking to him – so he wanted to know if they could do the

talking in her office. When she tried to refuse again, he threatened
to climb through the window.

In the end we managed to talk to her face to face for a few seconds.

Unfortunately it didn't help us get our hands on Daniel's travel permit. The next day when the South African embassy tried to
fax the affidavit, the fax machine in Avignon was out of order. A
day later the fax machine was working but it had run out of
paper. And the day after that the *préfecture* in Avignon was
closed. At the end of the week we boarded the plane to Cape
Town in blind faith that the entire family would be readmitted to
France.

The sequel to the story is that the French consulate in Cape
Town solved the nerve-racking problem in a day. Perhaps the
great distance between the diplomatic staff in Africa and the
fatherland allows them to be a little more lenient about official
papers. Perhaps it's just that things work differently in Africa.

And then at last it happened. Two years after I'd first applied for
a temporary residence permit I received an excited call from the
secretary at the local *mairie*. Come right away, Nathalie said,
your permit has arrived. As if it were an ice cream that would
melt if I didn't hurry. By this time the coveted bit of paper seemed
far less real than a melting ice cream, more like the Holy Grail. I
stuffed the baby into her pushchair and charged down the cobblestone lane so fast that the pushchair almost lost a wheel. Out of
breath I burst into the *mairie* and grabbed the laminated card out
of Nathalie's hand – and felt a wave of disappointment hit me.
Somewhere someone had made a mistake. It was my face in the
photo. It was my name on the card. But it couldn't be my permit.

I'd applied for a two-year permit that would have to be
renewed at regular intervals. (Before my arrival the French had
made it quite clear that this was the most I could hope for.) But
there was a very important condition attached to this bit of paper.
I wouldn't be allowed to work in France. Or rather, I'd be able to

work as a writer – not really regarded as *work*, I suppose – but trying to earn a French income was out of the question. And now I held in my shaking hands a ten-year residence permit, which gave me permission to work on top of it.

'They've made a mistake,' I muttered to Nathalie.

'Don't ask questions,' Nathalie said with a typically Gallic shrug. 'Take the permit and get out of here.'

Which is what I did.

But the next day I started asking questions all the same. Carefully, of French acquaintances, certainly not of French bureaucratic officials who might want to take the permit back. And that's how I discovered that the French government's unexpected generosity wasn't a miracle, just a practical arrangement for the sake of the baby in the pushchair with the broken wheel. I was no longer the undesirable *étrangère* from Africa; I was the mother of a French child. I'd earned a certain status. The French had opened their arms to me. And I wanted to tear off these arms with rage.

'Why didn't anyone tell me?!' I raged at the baby's French father. 'Surely they could see that I was pregnant every time I had to hand in another stupid piece of paper at the *préfecture*! And now I find out that all those papers were unnecessary!'

But Alain just shrugged, like Nathalie at the *mairie*, with a look that said, Don't ask questions.

5 Marry at leisure

'Shouldn't we just get married?' Alain asked one afternoon when I once again lay crying in a miserable bundle on the bed. 'It will at least solve a few of your problems with the bureaucracy.'

Not exactly what you'd call a romantic proposal, is it?

But at this stage nothing in my life was exactly romantic. I was living in the loveliest Provençal landscape, but I was so vehemently battling the French bureaucracy that I scarcely noticed the landscape. I was still hunting for official papers, and like any hunter worth his salt I had my eye on the prey rather than the scenery.

'It won't help,' I sobbed with red eyes and a wet nose. 'They won't give me a driver's licence just because I'm married to someone who has a driver's licence.'

For that was what this afternoon's crying bout was all about.

Well, actually it was about more than a driver's licence. Let's call it a cultural problem. National legislation leading to international misunderstandings. All symbolised by that shred of paper you need to drive a car.

I needed an insurance policy for the 15-year-old Golf I'd recently bought from a neighbour. The insurance company wasn't satisfied with the temporary international driver's licence

I'd managed with until now. If I wanted to insure the rusty little car with its torn seats, I needed a French driver's licence. But with this new French driver's licence I'd have to pay exorbitant monthly premiums on the policy – because as a 'new' driver I'd be considered a danger on the road.

I therefore had to prove that I'd been a responsible driver for two decades. All I needed was a photocopy of my twenty-year-old South African driver's licence. Did I say *all*? In the New South Africa the new government had just introduced a new system of driver's licences in the form of laminated cards. Therefore my South African driver's licence was also brand-new.

My previous driver's licence was, alas, in my previous identity document. This identity document had been replaced the previous year with the new identity document for which everyone in the New South Africa had to apply. In short, I had no proof that I'd been driving for years on some of the most dangerous roads in the world.

Of course I couldn't blame the French for the new laws of my fatherland. I'd simply have to put up and pay up.

But I did blame the French for refusing to issue my French driver's licence unless I relinquished my (brand-new! expensive!) South African driver's licence. I have to travel to South Africa regularly, sometimes at short notice, and over there I need a local driver's licence. The alternative, which is to apply for an international driver's licence every time I travel to South Africa, is too awful to contemplate. Here in France it's not a matter of quickly popping into the nearest AA office and walking out with your international driver's licence. Here you have to complete forms, as for anything you want to do here except go to the toilet (and for all I know you'll soon have to start completing forms for that), and then you have to wait. Sometimes for months on end.

It was this checkmate situation that made me sob my heart out that afternoon. And all it produced was a marriage proposal.

Of course it wasn't the first time that the word 'marry' had come up in our conversation. I'd moved to France boots and all because I was crazy about this man, but I'd resolved to get all my official papers in order, and only then we'd talk about marriage or no marriage. Just in case the man might think I was marrying him to make the paper trail easier.

But how was I to know that the paper trail would continue for more than two years? Or that in the meantime we would have a baby girl who would be crawling all over the house when I was still crawling around in front of French officials trying to get my hands on yet another essential document? To be completely honest, by now I didn't mind quite so much that my husband might one day reproach me because my reasons for marriage hadn't been entirely noble. I was beginning to think that I might be able to live with such a reproach.

And then my brother came to visit and Alain and I looked at each other and said, *pourquoi pas?* Why not pop over to the *mairie* and ask the mayor to marry us? Then at least I'd have a relative from South Africa as witness to the event.

Maybe I'd gone temporarily insane. Maybe I was imagining that I was living in Las Vegas where you could marry just like that, on the spur of the moment. Surely I should've known that no official transaction could be so effortless in this part of the world.

If I'd known how difficult it would be to arrange a simple wedding at the *mairie* – just the bridal pair and their children, I foolishly thought, just the briefest little ceremony imaginable – then I'd bloody well have remained unmarried.

Does anyone still remember the terrifying slogan for the movie *Jaws II*? *Just when you thought it was safe to go back into the water* … Indeed, just when I thought that it was safe to live in France, that there couldn't possibly be an official document left to complete, I decided to get married.

Then I was exposed to a new torrent of forms and papers.

One of the many requirements was a complete birth certificate

– requested from Pretoria and translated into French by an official translator – with a date stamp less than three months old. Sound familiar? Don't forget that I'd been on this absurd merry-go-round before when I had to prove that I was my own child's mother. By now I knew that it took three months to get your hands on such a certificate.

By which time my brother would have been back home, his French visit little more than a memory.

And if by some miracle the certificate arrived before the three-month deadline, we'd have to get married straightaway – no time to invite friends or family from afar – or we'd have to apply for the certificate again. And again hope in vain that it would reach us within three months. And again …

In the end we asked a family friend in Pretoria to collect the certificate in person and send it by express delivery, and so gained a week or three. But we were still rushing around to collect the rest of the papers.

As a prospective bride from a foreign country I needed, for example, to hand in a doctor's certificate at the *mairie*. The prospective groom wasn't expected to visit a doctor. It made no sense to me. *Why?* I wanted to know. Remember, by now I'd already given birth on French soil, and before I could do that, I was tested for every possible and impossible disease and complaint. The French really can be overly efficient when it comes to health.

But if I was found to be suffering from some mysterious condition that hadn't emerged during all those prenatal medical examinations, I asked Nathalie of the *mairie* – could the mayor refuse to marry me? Not as far as she knew, Nathalie said with her usual Gallic shrug. So what was the use of such a doctor's certificate? She wouldn't know, Nathalie said, she was just doing her job. Look, there it was on the official form, at the bottom of the extensive list of required documents: All foreign women under the age of 50 who want to marry in France have to submit a medical certificate.

Maybe it'll be easier to wait until you're fifty before you marry, was my brother's laconic comment.

I would be fifty anyway by the time I'd assembled the entire stack of papers, was how it seemed to me.

And when at last we walked into the *mairie*, triumphantly, with a plastic bag full of papers to set a date for the wedding, Nathalie's face fell as if she had to give us news of someone's death. The mayor wouldn't be able to marry us the coming Saturday. Or the next one. Nor probably on the Saturday after that. It was harvest time, you see, *les vendanges* as they call it in this wine region, and the mayor wasn't just the mayor. He was also the owner of a vineyard. And of the village's only wine cellar.

Les vendanges is something to experience in the French country-side. Because most of the farmers don't have permanent workers helping on their farms, every available body has to pitch in during the harvest. This means all the housewives in the village, all the unemployed men in the area, the adolescent children, the nephews and nieces. Even the barflies like Jean-Pierre tear themselves away from the bar counter for the sake of this communal task. (Not entirely without self-interest, since they're going to be drinking quite a lot of the wine that will be pressed from these grapes.) Hakima sends word that for a week or three she won't be able to come help in our house because she must help in the vineyard. (Unlike the barflies, she's doing it for purely economic reasons. Her Muslim family are about the only people in the village who don't drink wine.) Until a few years ago even Madame Voisine did her share – although she's so frail that you wonder how she ever managed to lift a basket of grapes. She was driven by neither economic reasons nor intemperance. She just did it out of curiosity. Now that she's too old to stand crouched all day long, she misses out on the juicy stories that are spread so literally through the grapevine.

Seasonal workers appear from every direction overnight.

Large families from Spain and the poorer East European countries, dark wandering gypsies and bored university students from
the cities, Rastafarians and backpackers, Algerians and other
North Africans. The green vineyards instantly turn into a kind of
United Nations, a confusion of tongues from the crack of dawn
till the sun sets, for seven days a week, until the last bunch has
been picked. And then, just as suddenly as the Babylonian business began, it's over. You wake up one morning to find all the seasonal workers gone, the housewives back in their houses,
Jean-Pierre back in the bar, and the vineyards empty and still.

Until next year.

I like the *vendanges*. I even feel a little melancholic every year
when it ends. But it isn't a good idea to get married during the
harvest – especially not if your mayor is a wine farmer. Even if
you managed with some effort to convince him to take a one-hour
break from the vineyard, there's still the risk that the official witnesses to your wedding ceremony won't arrive on time. Their car
will probably be delayed by the rows of tractors on their way to
the cellars with their wagonloads of grapes.

Our witnesses, two of Alain's colleagues, arrived so late that
we almost had to cancel the wedding. Our mayor, short and
round with a pair of wild black eyebrows and a head of black
hair standing permanently upright as if he's just been electro-
cuted, walked up and down impatiently and kept frowning at his
watch. There were still a lot of grapes to be picked that day.

And because France is France, we couldn't simply ask two
other friends (our only guests aside from our children) to take
over the role of official witnesses. Among the many forms we had
to complete beforehand, there were two for all the information
about our witnesses that you could think of: full names, where
and when and why they had been born, that sort of thing. In
other words: if your witnesses don't arrive, you might as well go
home to change out of your wedding dress and start filling in
forms again for permission to get married on another Saturday.

In our case that would definitely have been after the harvest.

The main reason why the mayor did after all agree to marry us on this inconvenient Saturday in September was that, for the first time in years, possibly decades, there had been two requests for wedding ceremonies. The other couple were, just like my less-than-radiant groom and me, not exactly spring chickens either. It was also a second wedding for them both and they also came to be wed in the presence of their children. The only difference was that they had more guests than children.

And oh yes, the other bride also looked decidedly more bridal than I did. She arrived in a smart hat, with a beautiful bouquet and a professionally made-up face. I was still feeding the baby half an hour before the wedding, with a dishcloth tied around my neck to keep my 'wedding gown' more or less clean. I'd bought the dress at a flea market a few days before – after briefly considering wearing the magnificent silk creation in which I'd embarked on my first marriage more than a decade earlier.

Like many inexperienced brides (you know better the second time round), I'd hung my designer wedding dress in a wardrobe years before in Cape Town, in the vague hope that it might one day enjoy another existence as an elegant evening gown. The problem was that I was never really invited to the kind of glamorous events where you'd need an elegant evening dress. A few literary award ceremonies were more or less the highlights of my social calendar, and a writer doesn't want to look like a bride when she's receiving a literary prize. Or worse, when she's not receiving the prize. So the wedding dress stayed in the wardrobe year after year.

When I moved to France, the wedding dress came along, partly for sentimental reasons, partly because I thought that it might finally be revived in another country, where no one knew my wedding dress or me. Alas, in the French countryside my social life was even more limited than in Cape Town. And after my daughter was born it disappeared completely. My second wedding therefore seemed like the very last chance I'd ever have to wear my beautiful wedding gown. Although I shuddered in advance at what any guide to etiquette would say of a bride who got married in the same dress twice.

And yet I knew from the start that it wouldn't work. You couldn't wear such an immodest dress to such a modest wedding. And I was determined that the wedding would be modest. My first marriage had begun with an impressive dress and ended with an impressive lawyer's bill. This time I would do it differently.

Besides, the groom didn't even own a tie, let alone a smart suit or a pair of suitable shoes.

However, my brother decided to lend his new brother-in-law a suit and, as my brother is also not really the suit-wearing type, it was a fairly flamboyant one with a collar of black brocade and a lining of scarlet satin, something that dated from London's Carnaby Street in the sixties. Such a wedding suit encouraged the groom's sense of the theatrical, and underneath the red satin lining he wore the frilly shirt he'd worn in an amateur theatre production a few months earlier.

It was therefore one of those rare weddings where the bride's outfit drew less attention than the groom's.

And because it was such a historical day for our little village, the local correspondent for the newspaper *La Provence* came to take our picture, which was published the following week under the headline, 'Two in one day'. The other couple's picture didn't appear along with ours, which unfortunately created the impression that Alain had married two women in one day. It led to many jokes in the local bar, particularly as we were surrounded in the picture by a crowd of children that couldn't possibly all belong to one woman. Besides the four children which Alain and I had brought into the world separately and together, there were also the two children of our official witnesses, plus a few of the village children who happened to be hanging around outside the *mairie* (probably because their mothers were all picking grapes), and who posed with us uninvited.

It certainly didn't resemble a traditional wedding picture, more like a children's choir with their two tired middle-aged chaperones.

I didn't mind. All that mattered was that all those months of filling out forms and signing papers were finally over.

Or that's what I thought. Soon afterwards we decided to buy a house. And then the paper chase started all over again ...

6   I'm on strike

It's a long weekend, a summery long weekend in the south of France. The sun is shining in its high blue heaven, the cherries glisten like rubies in the cherry orchards, the first plump melons of the season lie in stacks of glowing green and yellow on the market. Nothing to complain of, thank you, it's just that ...

Well, the children are not exactly excited about the long weekend. The teachers and other educational staff have been striking intermittently for several weeks, so the children are at home more often than they are at school anyway. To Daniel it seems as if the long summer vacation has started two months early this year. Marvellous for the children, less marvellous for parents like me who cannot work because I have to look after the children day in and day out.

But I'm not complaining. I support the educationists' cause. It's just that ...

My husband was supposed to take our daughter to his family in Lille for the long weekend. To bond a little with her French grandparents and cousins, and to give me a badly needed breather after weeks of babysitting during school hours. Yesterday he heard that they couldn't go because the trains were on strike (as were the planes, the buses, the trams and the subway). It's too far to travel by car – but even if it were closer, they couldn't have gone by road because the truck drivers are on strike. And truck drivers, as everyone in France knows, don't play around with people in small cars. They obstruct the highways and the access routes to cities and that's that. You don't argue with a truck that weighs a couple of tons and has about ten wheels.

But let's assume that my husband and daughter reached Lille by some miraculous means – by borrowing Harry Potter's broomstick, or mounting a winged horse, something like that – then my troubles would still not be over. I wouldn't know for example which clothes to pack for Mia. Short pants or long? Sandals or gumboots? I usually just turn on the radio and listen to the weather forecast for the entire country – but now the radio is also on strike. The official TV stations aren't on strike (yet), but I'm terribly confused about the programmes because our weekly TV guide hasn't been delivered. You see, the post office is on strike.

The banks were on strike last week, and will be again next week, so I must remember to make sure that I have enough cheques in my cheque book and cash in my purse to handle a possible emergency. The doctors and other medical personnel are fortunately not on strike at the moment (they were, a few months ago, on a grand scale), except for those who are involved in the education system, like school nurses. The only ray of light in this general chaos, as far as I can see, is that the income tax office is also on strike. Hopefully this means that Alain will not be fined this year for being late with his tax forms as usual.

No, I'm not complaining. I'm just saying. 'Welcome to the First World', I keep telling myself. And be grateful that you're not living a little further to the south in Marseille. There the garbage removal workers have been on strike for weeks now. And because the entire region has been hit by an extraordinary heat wave, you need a gas mask to make it past the stinking rubbish bags in the streets. The rats are out in droves and residents fear an outbreak of horrible medieval diseases.

This is France in the year 2003. Not that I want to run down the country. Different countries have different problems.

It reminds me of a story that I read a year ago or so in Oom Krisjan Lemmer's column in the *Mail and Guardian*, a humorous way of explaining the economies of different countries in terms of two cows. For example: the American owns two cows and has them milked twelve hours a day – and then is terribly indignant when both collapse and die. The Englishman has two cows and they're both mad. The Italian has two cows, but he can't find them. And the Frenchman? He's on strike because he wants three cows.

If you lived here, you'd find it funny.

If you don't find it funny, you should perhaps consider going to live in America or England instead.

Not a single week goes by without some group of workers in France being on strike. Whether you're a street-sweeper or a street-walker, strike you will. Recently, even the hairdressers were on strike. In protest against heaven knows what, they covered the famous Champs Elysées in Paris with a carpet of hair. Hair that had been cut and shaved from the heads of thousands of clients. Even rural hairdressers participated in the protest. With bags full of hair they caught the train for Paris. Our local hairdresser wasn't there, so I cannot claim that I (or my hair) was involved in this hair-raising action.

Perhaps not quite as effective as blockading the Champs Elysées with trucks but a lot more imaginative.

Strikes are more than a tradition here, they're a way of life, and the French are mostly surprisingly tolerant of this disruptive social phenomenon. '*Bof*,' says Jean-Pierre and rubs his moustache philosophically: 'I don't dare complain if you're on strike because next month it's my turn.' Which makes me wonder. Going on strike means that you stop doing something – and what does Jean-Pierre actually *do*? Apart from sitting in the bar?

Madame Voisine, I've been surprised to learn, was for years an active member of the local Communist Party, a leader in many strike actions and protest marches. I'd judged her as too light-weight (literally and figuratively) for weighty matters like politics.

Which just goes to show. You can't judge a book by its cover. Even when the cover is as colourful as this Provençal parrot. Now that Madame Voisine's husband is often poorly, she seems to consider it her duty to care for him rather than range herself on the side of the world's workers. But the moment Monsieur is no longer there, the widow Voisine's insatiable curiosity will in all likelihood lead her to a few more protest marches. Such a nice convivial way of finding out what's going on in other people's lives. Until then she'll just have to be content with the regular funeral processions in the village.

Of course some strikes are more trying than others. The truck drivers remain the big bullies on this playground. A few years ago, in protest against a petrol price increase, they surrounded all the petrol reservoirs. Within days it became impossible to buy a drop of fuel anywhere in the country. It was one of the many potential catastrophes that loomed over my wedding day. Right up to the last minute we weren't sure if our witnesses would have enough petrol to get them to the ceremony.

This is why I don't want to complain about the current wave of strikes. It's apparently the biggest one to hit the country in a decade, a veritable tidal wave of protest, but by now I'm starting to get used to it.

Of all the strikes I've personally experienced, the most trying – and simultaneously also the most absurd – was when everyone ran out of money. The workers responsible for the transport of money to and from banks – those armed guys in their impressive armoured cars – had gone on strike. Within days there were cash-flow problems throughout the country. The ATMs were empty, your local bank couldn't change your cheques into money, your local shop couldn't give you change. When buying your daily *baguette* at the bakery, or three apples and a head of lettuce at the market, you had to write out a cheque. In another few days no one had any cheques left. Soon credit cards became the only method of payment. Imagine. Every time you ordered a cup of coffee at a café, you had to haul out your card.

When the strike ended, we had a good laugh about it. But while it lasted, while you didn't know when next you'd feel a *centime* between your fingers, it was quite a terrifying experience.

Sometimes, just now and again, I wish that I could also go on strike. It's not that I want to disrupt the entire country. Just a humble little strike in and around the house. Just a day or three of refusing to touch the laundry, the dishes, dirty floors or unmade beds. Maybe I could stand under the plane tree with a placard and shout a few slogans to draw the attention of the neighbours. Maybe one of them would even call the local paper.

Surely it should be newsworthy. Even in this strike-mad country I've never heard of a striking mother. Nor a striking writer, come to think of it.

I might actually be the only adult in France who has never taken part in a strike.

This tale has meanwhile grown a little tail. Stories about strikes often grow little tails and these little tails grow little tails of their own, because like the poor the strikers will always be among us. While I'm writing this, there is a strike among French diplomatic staff. Not just countrywide but, given the nature of their work, worldwide. French embassies and consulates all over the world are locked or abandoned. It's an amazing first, even for a country where strikes are a national pastime.

After all, the work of diplomats is to defend their country's policy, however senseless that policy might seem to the rest of the world. And now French diplomats are protesting, in a decidedly undiplomatic way, against their government's policy to cut the diplomatic budget.

Put another way, French diplomats are on strike because they want three cows.

7 Doctor, doctor

Maybe doctors everywhere are a strange species. Maybe I just didn't realise it in South Africa because there I lived alone in astonishingly good health.

Now that I've become part of a family of six – what the French call *une famille nombreuse*, a numerous family – doctors have become a part of everyday life. Now I look back with nostalgia at the friendly, helpful and above all familiar doctors of my native land. Familiar as in, they understand your language, you understand their ways.

The first time I ended up at a French doctor, after barely a month in the country, I was a nervous wreck. Firstly because I couldn't remember the French word for toenail and here I had to explain the painful history of an ingrown toenail in French. I'd lost the nail of my big toe a few months earlier, as the result of a gruelling hiking trip in the Fish River Canyon, and the new nail wouldn't grow out right. Or rather, grew in instead of out.

Secondly because, once I was inside the doctor's surgery, I had to compete with a telephone that rang every two minutes. Every time I managed to come up with a broken phrase in French, the phone rang on the doctor's desk. Then she answered it, made appointments, dispensed medical advice, listened to the complaints of hypochondriac patients. It was a revelation that doctors could manage without secretaries or receptionists. And it was endlessly frustrating to have to keep starting my bungling French explanation from scratch.

After half an hour I'd still not made it to the examination table, had not even removed my shoe to show the doctor my objectionable toenail. All I'd really done was to sit opposite the desk fully clothed and listen to the doctor talk to other patients. Once every few minutes I had the chance to say something. Then the doctor's impatient frown made it immediately clear that she hadn't understood a word. And then, before I could try again, the telephone rang.

I would've loved to storm out of the surgery in a rage. But where would that get me? I would've had to explain from scratch, to another doctor, who would probably also constantly answer the phone.

I was beginning to grasp how things worked around here.

In the end she didn't even look at the toenail. She summarily referred me to a specialist at a hospital – and wrote me a bill. Which I had to pay there and then. Another shock. Where I come from, the bill arrives only a month later. Doctors don't compromise their dignity by asking for money across the desk. That's the secretary's job! Like answering the phone!

These days I'm not so easily shocked by French doctors. I now know that you cannot make an appointment to see your GP at half past ten in the morning and reasonably expect to be sitting inside his surgery around eleven. No, you go early in the morning, as soon as the surgery opens, and you wait your turn. In a waiting room, with no receptionist, among a horde of other patients. It can take hours before you get to the doctor. With a sick child moaning in your arms, among other moaning sick children, every one of those hours can feel like a month.

To see more specialised doctors – dermatologists, gynaecologists, paediatricians and so on – you can make an appointment for a specific time. In theory, then, you'll be seeing the doctor at half past ten. But in practice you usually still have to wait an hour or more in a crowded waiting room.

Sometimes, however, there is the exception that proves the rule. One day I staggered into a dentist's waiting room five minutes late, after the babysitter dropped me and I had to phone around urgently to find someone else to look after the baby, and there the dentist stood waiting for me with folded arms. And before I could mumble an apology, she addressed me in the tones of a headmaster reprimanding a naughty child: 'The appointment was for three o'clock, madame. Not for five past three.'

I know. I could've told her where to stick her appointment. I could've gone to find another dentist. But my French wasn't fluent enough for bitchy remarks. I just bit my tongue and opened my mouth so that she could do her job.

Humility is one of the virtues I've gained in the French countryside.

Particularly in my negotiations with doctors. Let me add right away that there are also some wonderful doctors here. Kind souls with patient faces and good manners. But for some or other reason I more frequently end up with doctors who are dour, bossy or just plain rude. The dermatologist to whom I took my daughter to have a rare kind of wart removed from her foot began the session by taking me to task because the child was still in nappies at the age of two. I was so surprised at this audacity – cobbler, stick to your last! – that I merely gaped at her.

The fact that all three of the abovementioned doctors were female has nothing to do with the price of eggs. At least, I hope not. As a loyal member of the female gender, I really hope not. But just to put matters into perspective, let me publicly declare that the rudest doctor I've ever had to deal with was a man, a leading optometrist in the region, who seemed to think that his patients were too weak-sighted to notice his rudeness. Ah well, I told myself after the first visit, a good bedside manner isn't everything, is it? Give the man a chance. Even the best doctors have their bad days. The second time I realised that the previous time had been a *good* day for him. After that I preferred to drive two hours more to an optometrist in another city.

It was Madame Voisine who referred me to the second optometrist. Like almost all the French people I know, she's a bit of a hypochondriac. They visit the doctor much too often and they use far too much medicine. But then, I am a Calvinist who was raised with the idea that pain and suffering are a part of life, our punishment for our forefathers' sins. The Mediterranean Catholics around here seem to take a different view. You don't suffer in silence, you rush to the nearest doctor and swallow everything that he gives you to swallow.

In addition to which I've never met a doctor anywhere else who'll give you as much to swallow as the average French doctor. No prescription ever consists of a single little tablet or ointment. No, the doctor plays it safe and prescribes four different tablets. One of the four is bound to have the desired effect.

And I'm not just talking from personal experience. My suspicion was officially confirmed on TV the other night. Research and opinion surveys have shown that the French drink far more medicine than, say, the Dutch or the Germans.

Madame Voisine will proudly tell you that the French public health service and medical insurance are among the best in the world. Better even than those of the Scandinavian countries! *Quelle chance!* She probably considers it her patriotic duty to use as much of these world-famous services as possible. If Madame Voisine has a runny nose, she wouldn't dream of blowing it until she's been to a doctor to find out exactly how and when and where it must be blown.

But most of the time the doctors in France make me feel bewildered rather than cross, purely because things are done differently from what I'm used to. Like the first time I went to a gynaecologist and was asked to remove my clothes. In some embarrassment I went behind a transparent little curtain to look for (a) a hanger for my clothes and (b) a little gown or other bit of clothing to cover my shame. No hanger. No shred of cloth to place over the necessary bits.

Yes, everyone knows that it's a gynaecologist's job to look at naked women, but where I come from, allowances are made for the woman's embarrassment. You're not expected to stride stark naked through the surgery to step onto a scale. In South Africa the scale is usually behind the curtain so the woman can cheat if she wants to. And show me the woman who doesn't sometimes want to cheat when she gets onto a scale.

My current gynaecologist doesn't even have a little curtain you can hide behind. The first time I had to shed my clothes, I opened the first door I could see, thinking it had to be a changing room, and found myself looking inside the broom cupboard. Oh no, the gynaecologist laughed, she didn't have a changing room, she was an anarchist.

No, don't ask me what anarchy has to do with changing rooms. Or why an anarchistic gynaecologist would keep six brooms in her surgery.

Don't ask me anything about French doctors. I'm still struggling to fit all the pieces into the puzzle.

Not that I lack opportunities to work on the puzzle. With four children in the house you end up at the doctor four times more often than if you had just one. When three of them are rough boys who fall out of trees and from roofs, have accidents with skateboards and bicycles, or just fall on the frozen street right outside the house and lose a few teeth, you spend more time in a doctor's waiting room than most people could handle.

When South African journalists ask me what my hobbies are here in France, I usually say something appropriate like walking or eating delicious food. But actually it is to wait for medical treatment. When I'm asked about my dreams for the future, I mutter something about the wonderful book I'm one day going to write. But really my immediate dream is to get through just one school holiday without a sick or injured child.

It's such a humble desire, isn't it? Didn't I tell you that life in the French countryside has made me humble?

8   Born in three languages

I should've known that it was too good to be true. The pregnancy was going just too smoothly. That is not how things work. Not in my life. Not this sort of thing.

It was one of those unplanned, late-in-life pregnancies. 'Geriatric' is the unflattering medical term. At least I was less 'geriatric' than Princess Caroline of Monaco, or the British prime minister's wife, Cherie Blair, who were both expecting late-born babies along with me. That was how I consoled myself at night, when the size of my tummy began to make sleep impossible.

The fact that this to-do was taking place abroad had me very worried. I felt completely lost, far from my mother's advice and my friends' support, abandoned to doctors with strange surnames (Taouk and Zerafa were my two medical guardian angels) who did everything differently from what I was used to.

And then there was the language problem. My French had indeed improved since I'd come to live in the French countryside, but my vocabulary was still restricted to the small talk you make with the baker when buying your *baguette*. The wind that's been blowing for nine days now, a nasty cold, your child's school. I certainly wasn't equal to complicated gynaecological or paediatric discussions. What if I swallowed the wrong pill, what if I did something incredibly stupid, just because I'd misunderstood the doctor?

And then everything went so well that one by one my fears disappeared. When on top of it all the amniocentesis confirmed that a little girl was on the way, Alain and I were completely lightheaded with joy. We adored our three sons, but we'd both been dreaming of a daughter all our lives. And for me, as the only female in the house (except for the dog), the testosterone levels were sometimes overwhelming. My daughter would be my ally in this undeclared war between genders. Oestrogen rules, OK?

Our biggest problem at this stage was finding a name that could be pronounced the same way in Afrikaans, French, English or any other language our cosmopolitan daughter might one day want to speak. After all I'd heard how Alain's French family destroyed my name – Marita van der Vyver became *Magite vah de Vivah* – and how my Afrikaans family struggled with his name and those of his sons. In French Alain is pronounced *Aláng*, Thomas is *Tommah* and Hugo is *Ighó*. Try and explain that to your uncle in Upington. My friend Koos gave up after three days and started calling Alain *Elaine*. Alain still calls Koos *Quees*. Fortunately Daniel's name is commonly known in France. They pronounce it completely differently but unlike me he doesn't have to spell his name from beginning to end every time he introduces himself.

That's why we decided to call our daughter Mia. Even in Chinese Mia would sound like Mia. No problems, I thought.

That was before I realised how conservative the French still are when it comes to names.

Basically you stick to the three hundred-odd names found on the Roman Catholic calendar of name days – and some of those are genuinely odd, like Guénolé on March 3 or Fiacre on August 30. I have never met a Guénolé or a Fiacre. Nor has Alain. But naming my daughter Fiacre would probably have caused less consternation every time I introduce her.

'*Mia?!?*' That's the reaction I keep getting. Eyebrows are raised, foreheads creased, eyes display utter incomprehension. And then comes the inevitable question. The one question I

thought I would avoid when I gave my daughter a name that consisted of only three letters. 'How do you spell it?'

Now I know. If your name isn't on that calendar, or otherwise
a universally recognised French word, let's say a flower name like
Iris or Rose, you're going to spend a lifetime struggling to introduce yourself. No, there is another exception. In the past decade
or two it has become fashionable to give your child an American
name – usually inspired by popular TV series or movie stars – like
Sue Ellen and Pamela and Kevin and Bruce. The trouble is that
these names are hopelessly mangled by the average French
tongue. I've already met a host of *Kêveen*s aged between ten and
fifteen, and almost as many *Bgoose*s. Having said that, any alternative to Bruce is probably an improvement.

Perhaps the next decade will see a popular American TV series
with a Mia in the leading role. I would hate anyone to think that
I'd named my daughter after a TV character – but it will make my
Mia's social life a lot easier.

When I was pregnant, of course, all these name shocks lay in the
future. I waited for the birth of my daughter in blissful ignorance
and glowing health. By the eighth month there was a warning
that the baby might be born early if I didn't get as much rest as
possible. A good excuse not to wash the dishes, I thought. As you
will have noticed by now, I'll grab any excuse to avoid washing
the dishes. By the ninth month I began to believe that I'd been
quite unnecessarily neurotic. No, I recklessly declared, giving
birth in a strange country isn't nearly as bad as you'd think.

Until the final medical appointment – four weeks before the
anticipated birth date – when the doctor told Alain and me
almost casually that Alain wouldn't be allowed to attend the
birth. Our babbling excitement instantly made way for speechless
dismay.

In the preceding months we'd carefully discussed every possible potential problem with the doctor. Alain accompanied me to
every medical appointment, initially because I needed an inter-

preter, but later – as my French vocabulary grew to encompass terms such as muscle spasms and haemorrhoids and varicose veins and other gruesome details of pregnancy – purely because he wanted to share the experience with me. We knew that the baby would be born by epidural caesarean, like my son eight years before in Cape Town. The doctor had explained the procedure to us step by step so that I could be certain that it would be done the same way as in South Africa. We had visited the hospital's labour ward, met the nursing staff, even made an appointment with the anaesthetist. The one issue we'd never raised – because we took it for granted – was the father's presence at the birth.

Which is why I could only gape at the doctor when he told us at the eleventh hour that the father wouldn't be allowed inside the theatre. It sounded positively medieval! Not for a caesarean, the doctor explained when he saw the shocked expression on my face. For a normal birth the father could be there, but not for a caesarean.

'But in South Africa ...' I stammered.

'Not in France,' the doctor said.

'But in Britain and America and other countries ...'

'Not in France,' the doctor repeated. Not unsympathetically.

Alain and I looked at each other in despair. He wanted to be present when his daughter was born – and I wanted him to share this experience with me. Besides, I was simply too terrified to do it on my own. I'd always been scared of hospitals, and a hospital in a strange country, with staff that spoke a strange language, was a phantom out of my worst nightmare.

I burst into tears from sheer frustration, as I so often do here in France. Because I can't understand how things work. Because there seems to be some code operating that I just cannot crack. Because I'd been stupid enough to believe that a French birth would be the same as a South African one – only in another language.

Alain stayed calm and with a determined look asked if there

was a doctor anywhere in France who would allow him to watch his daughter being born. By all appearances he was prepared to launch a countrywide search, to advertise in newspapers and on the radio if need be. 'Wanted: A sympathetic obstetrician willing to accommodate an anxious father ...'

Well, the doctor said, and thought for a moment. He didn't want to raise our hopes, but ... He wrote a name on a piece of paper. A colleague, not very far from here, who'd studied in Britain and worked in Canada. Asking him couldn't do any harm. With his English background, who knew?

A weak flame of hope was lit in my heart.

I waited three days for an appointment with this obstetrician. The fact that the baby was still threatening to put in an early appearance made those three days seem like three lifetimes. I was afraid to move and swallowed a pill every few hours to delay the contractions. But when at last I sat in his surgery and explained my despair, he immediately set my mind at ease, in perfect English, which was a fantastic bonus after months of broken conversations with the previous doctor. The father was welcome in his theatre, he assured me.

Big sigh of relief.

That was, if the anaesthetist didn't ban the father.

The weak flame sputtered and went out.

He worked with two anaesthetists, the doctor explained. One would admit Alain, the other one would probably refuse. But it wasn't the end of the world, he tried to comfort me. We just had to plan the operation for when the 'right' anaesthetist would be on duty.

I was in no way comforted. What would happen if the baby arrived before the planned date? When the wrong anaesthetist was on duty? Or on a day when the right anaesthetist but the wrong obstetrician was on duty? After all, babies were inclined to arrive when they did, not when you planned it. And the fact that my previous pregnancy had ended a good three weeks early didn't augur well.

But with this doctor Alain at least had a chance of watching his daughter being born. And a girl would probably have better timing, as a friend wrote from South Africa. She'd be polite enough to wait until the hostess was ready before rocking up at the party.

And then, ten days before the planned date, we were hit by the worst snowstorm this region had seen in decades. Within hours all the roads around our village became completely impassable, the highways were obstructed, the electricity was cut. And suddenly the possibility that Alain might miss his daughter's birth was no longer my worst fear. Suddenly there was the terrifying possibility that he might have to help bring the baby into the world – in a house without power, by flickering candle-light, with a pot of water brought to boil in the fireplace.

For days the snow lay at calf-height around our house. We began to put emergency measures in place, like asking the American neighbour if we might borrow his four-wheel-drive to try and get me to hospital. And I paged through medical books, with growing despair, to study home-birthing techniques.

When at last the snow began to melt – when the first car in days roared past the house – I began to understand how Noah must have felt in his ark when he saw that green twig in the dove's beak.

In the end the girl was indeed considerate enough to stay inside until the planned date – for which she has my eternal gratitude. No shock, no labour pains, no nerve-racking rush to reach the labour ward in time. We could drive to the hospital calmly the night before. I was monitored the entire night via every machine imaginable, loaded onto a trolley early the next morning and pushed into the theatre.

Alain sat on a high chair to the left of my head and held my hand so tightly that it almost cut off my circulation, but I didn't complain. I was only too grateful that he was there.

When the theatre sister greeted me in English – with a beautiful British accent – I was completely stunned. I hadn't quite expected an English-speaking medical team to be arranged specially for me. No, the doctor explained, amused, it was mere coincidence that this nurse – who had worked in Britain for more than a decade – was on duty today.

And so the strange operation began – the lower half of my body in the capable hands of the English-speaking doctor and sister, the top half equally capably cared for by the 'right' French anaesthetist who didn't understand a single English sentence. And by my left ear, my beloved Alain, muttering words of comfort in both languages.

Less than an hour later I heard my daughter's bellowing voice for the first time. A big and healthy baby, a whole 4,23 kg, rosy and noisy. When the sister handed her to me, I saw a fat crumpled little face below a shock of dark hair. After that my eyes were too full of tears to see anything.

'Welcome here with us, Mia,' I whispered. In Afrikaans. So that one day I would be able to tell her that she was born in three languages.

9   Stranger than fiction

The people who read my books would like to believe that I lead a charmed life. A fairytale come true, and in Provence at that. And the more I declare that my life is really rather dull and boring, except that is for the endless domestic catastrophes of an over-sized family, the less they believe me.

All right, I concede that when I write to my friends about spending the last weekend at the famous film festival in Cannes, it might sound impressive. As if I'd casually waved to Catherine Deneuve or Nicole Kidman in passing. Alas.

I've been in Cannes during the film festival two or three times now, because it's close enough for a day trip, because it's more exciting than Oudtshoorn during the arts festival, and because I've never seen so many limousines in one day anywhere else, not even around Central Park in New York. But I've never seen any famous movie stars up close. I lack the patience to hang around for hours among the crowds outside the stars' hotels. I find it much more interesting to stare at the people who've come to stare at the stars.

I did catch a glimpse of Johnny Depp's hair once. I happened to be walking past his hotel at just the right moment. And I once saw Robin Williams's profile in a sports car. Well actually I didn't realise that it was Robin Williams I was looking at until the woman next to me fainted.

The crowds who converge on Cannes to catch a fleeting glimpse of a hero's nose remind me of the faithful who stream to Lourdes to experience a miracle – the same suppressed hysteria, fanatic hope, fantastic patience. The same excess of kitsch souvenirs, too.

I experience Cannes on an entirely different level. The last time I went there was with Daniel, Mia and my brother from South Africa. We took a picnic basket because during the festival a cup of coffee and a croissant cost roughly the same as a three-course meal at a decent restaurant in South Africa. We ate our modest sandwiches under a palm tree next to the beach. Not the exclusive bits of fenced-off beach where the rich and famous lie around in deck chairs, just an ordinary beach open to everyone. I paged through the Sunday paper, Daniel and Mia played in the shallow waves, my brother looked at the bare breasts of the women on the beach. After a while he sighed and asked why only the old ones and the fat ones removed their tops. In other words we could just as well have been sitting on the beach at Laaiplek. The waves would've been bigger, the water colder, the bare breasts fewer. I can't really think of any other difference.

Afterwards we did wander through the crowds, admired the limousines and the luxury yachts in the harbour, and listened to the faithful scream every time some body-part of a star came into sight somewhere. It's a strange sound, impossible to ignore, almost like a bomb siren in wartime. After hearing such rousing screams for an entire day, you are inevitably left with a bit of adrenaline pumping through your veins.

That's my experience of Cannes. Excitement at a distance. Just enough to make me return to my rather dull and boring existence with contentment, even relief.

But sometimes, quite unexpectedly, I do experience a sort of glamorous glory here in Provence. Usually it happens at stations and airports. Nothing to do with the romance of farewells and departures – just more proof, perhaps, of how limited my social life is here. When I do go out, the destination is often a station or airport – to pick up or drop off a child, friend or relative.

At Avignon station, for example, I ran into the American movie star John Malkovich. Not once, but twice. And not during the annual arts festival in Avignon either. During the festival you might expect to see a few international stars – although they don't usually hang around at the station. Celebrities as you know don't really use public transport. No, these were just ordinary station days. And suddenly this vision in a white linen suit stood before me, a white Panama hat on his head, eyes humbly downcast.

The first time I thought I was hallucinating. Two weeks earlier I'd watched the movie *Being John Malkovich*, an imaginative story in which nearly all the characters turn into clones of the actor John Malkovich. No, not clones exactly, they actually become John Malkovich, but it's hopelessly too complicated to explain here. Fact is, when soon afterwards I found myself face to face with the real John Malkovich, I thought that the movie had affected my mind. Movies sometimes have a strange effect on my imagination.

Besides, no one else at the station batted an eyelid or showed a hint of surprise. No sign of the hysterical screams that an actor of this standing would've drawn in Cannes. The only possible conclusion, if you ruled out hallucination, was that no one else had recognised him. After all, who on earth expects to see John Malkovich at the magazine kiosk on a station in the French countryside?

Any other American movie star would probably have caused a stir, surrounded by muscular bodyguards and personal trainers and fawning assistants. I can't imagine Bruce Willis, say, waiting patiently and alone in line to pay for a newspaper. But that's probably one of the reasons why I have a greater admiration for John Malkovich than for, say, Bruce Willis.

Believe me, as he stood there waiting in his linen suit, he was a model of old-world elegance and civilised reserve among all the scruffy, noisy, impatient travellers on the station. I joined the queue beside him, just to make completely sure that I wasn't dealing with a clone from a movie script, and tried to keep from hyperventilating.

Alain was terribly amused and took great pleasure in repeating the story, with a good deal of exaggeration, to several friends. In his version I jumped up and down uttering little screams of ecstasy. Not true, I promise. I maintain that I conducted myself with great dignity in trying circumstances. But whichever version you choose to believe, the fact that I would make such a fuss over an unexpected encounter at a station must prove beyond a shadow of a doubt that my life in the French countryside doesn't exactly overflow with excitement.

The second time I spotted the actor he was on the opposite platform, waiting for a train. This time I wanted to remain cool as a cucumber. Just to show Alain.

'There's Malkovich again,' I muttered to my friend in vaguely bored tones.

'*What?*' she exclaimed. '*John Malkovich?*'

'Yes!' I giggled. 'John Malkovich!'

As cool as curry.

And then there was the time I took my dad to the airport at Marseille. I didn't run into a movie star, but I nearly became one myself.

While I was having a cup of coffee at the airport café, a handsome young man suddenly knelt next to my chair and asked if I was interested in acting in a movie. Now had I been twenty years younger I might have been annoyed at such a clumsy pick-up line. But at my ripe age I could only stare at him in confusion.

Wait, he said, let him explain. And he whipped out a business card with the name of a movie company on it. I instantly thought of those TV programmes that make fools of people in front of hidden cameras. Looked about me suspiciously, and then asked straight out if it was a joke.

No, he assured me, he worked for Robert Guediguian – a

director from Marseille who was so well known that even I had heard of him – and they were looking for a tall blonde woman for a wedding scene in his next film. In Marseille, where all the women are small and dark, it was a hopeless quest. It was despair that made him hang around the airport in the hope of finding a tall blonde woman from elsewhere.

I had of course noticed that the people of Marseille didn't resemble those from Amsterdam or Stockholm. But I hadn't realised that I was such a freak here in the south that purely on the strength of my height (and I'm not even exceptionally tall) and my hair (which is also not exceptionally blonde), I'd be begged to appear in a movie. Because by now the young man was begging. On his knees, literally, beside me.

The fact that I couldn't speak proper French in no way discouraged him. For the small part he had in mind, I'd only have to say a few sentences. And if that didn't work out, my voice could always be dubbed.

It was flattering, I admit, being begged to appear in a movie by a handsome young man. I gave him my telephone number and allowed him to take my Polaroid picture. Over dinner that night I regaled my family with the story. *The day Mom almost became a movie star.* Thomas regarded me with amusement while he played with his long ponytail. You could tell he was thinking this was probably something I'd invented, like the stories in my books.

The next day brought another domestic crisis, Hugo and Daniel playing with matches next to the gas bottle in the bathroom and nearly blowing up the lot of us, if I remember correctly. Something, at any rate, that made me forget all about my moment of glory at the airport.

So imagine my surprise when the talent scout called me two weeks later to say that they'd finally found a French-speaking actress for the part. He thanked me politely for my willingness and asked if he could keep the Polaroid picture in their files. In case they needed someone like me in the future. In other words: a tall blonde woman who spoke bad French. No, that wasn't what he said, it was what I thought.

And then I once again forgot the whole thing – until about a year later when a woman phoned from another film company in Marseille to say that she might have a small part for me. Funny, eh? In all my years in South Africa, where I could speak at least two languages perfectly, no one ever offered me a part in anything. And here I was in the French countryside, a middle-aged housewife with a language problem, and suddenly I was inundated with talent scouts who wanted to make me a movie star.

On that occasion the woman wanted a recent picture of me in a standing position, probably to check that I wasn't too fat or too thin or too whatever. Problem: I don't have a single recent picture of me standing alone. I am a mother, remember. I have several pictures where I'm posing with a baby in my arms or a child attached to my hand, visibly exhausted the way mothers usually look in pictures, and a typical holiday snap where I'm standing next to a camel in Egypt. So I sent her two pictures – one with a child and one with a camel.

I never heard from her again. I guess she had something more professional in mind.

But somewhere in an office in Marseille there is to this day a file with a Polaroid of a tallish, blondish woman drinking coffee at an airport. Who knows, maybe the camel picture and the child picture have been added to the file. Who knows if these three pictures might not one day launch my French film career?

Don't laugh. Stranger things have happened since I've lived here. For example I ran into John Malkovich at the station.

In the south of France, as in all Mediterranean regions, there are a couple of dead hours in every day. The morning has barely ended, the nearest church bell has yet to cough twelve times, when bakers and bankers and bureaucrats and other working souls start to lock their doors. By noon businesses and civil service offices are deserted. Only in another four hours or so will the first signs of life re-appear.

We're talking of course about that vital institution, *la sieste*. An hour of rest while the sun is at its hottest. Four hours of rest, actually, although no one sleeps for four hours. It's a case of three hours of non-stop eating and drinking – at the end of which anyone would need a break before resuming the daily grind.

If you're living in Provence, the idea of a quick sandwich between one and half past before you return to duty is so senseless that only the Americans could've invented it.

Even at school the children are served a four-course meal every day. Starter, main course, cheese, dessert. In that order. The opposite of fast food. Slow food. Truck drivers have a four-course meal in a restaurant – and then they nap inside their trucks before they drive on. Shopkeepers and tradesmen often go home for lunch – and then they sleep in their own beds before they return to work.

When I first came to live here, this black hole in the middle of the day drove me mad. Okay, it makes sense in summer when it's too hot between twelve and four to do anything anyway, but in the heart of winter? In winter the middle of the day is the best time to get anything done. Before twelve it is too dark or too cold. After four it is too dark or too cold. And between twelve and four you find yourself outside one deserted building after another.

That first winter in Provence I attempted an enthusiastic sightseeing tour of a different village every Sunday. And Sunday after Sunday at noon I was wandering through hamlets as silent as the grave. Not a soul on the street, not a dog that barked, every door and shutter closed. Nothing but the sad wind blowing. *High Noon*. That's what I kept being reminded of. All those cowboy movies where a stranger walks down the dusty main street of an apparently deserted town. Just tumbleweed tumbling in the distance.

I know Provence isn't the Wild West. I've never seen tumbleweed around here. I'm talking about the general atmosphere of a tiny village between twelve and four on a wintry Sunday, when you feel like the only survivor of a nuclear explosion.

I've now lived here long enough to plan my Sundays better. In winter we stay at home like everyone else. In summer our excursions start early in the morning before it gets too hot. Or after four, when the worst heat is over.

You learn to compromise. You learn to wait, to be patient, to be tranquil.

When it comes to patience I still have a long way to go. But I have also covered quite a distance. For example, I can now stand in line in a village supermarket along with all the other customers listening to the owner's telephone conversation with a distant relation, about another distant relation's haemorrhoid operation, without wanting to explode with impatience.

While this conversation is going on, the shop is at a standstill. After all, Madame Coccimarket cannot talk on the phone and work the cash register at the same time. But all the customers wait meekly while the haemorrhoid operation is described in the finest detail. Sometimes they join in the conversation, commenting on the distant relation's medical problem and telling everyone who wants to listen (or not) about their own medical problems.

If Madame Voisine happens to be in the queue, you can expect a lively conversation. And she's in the queue with astonishing regularity. Just as you can't walk into the local bar without encountering Jean-Pierre, you usually can't walk into the local shop without running into Madame Voisine.

Interestingly enough, you will also, by way of exception, sometimes find Madame Voisine in the bar, enjoying a quick coffee with her neighbours. But I've yet to see Jean-Pierre in the supermarket. Don't ask me where Jean-Pierre buys his food. Of if he ever buys food. He's not starving, if his paunch is anything to go by. But what and where and with whom he eats remains a dark secret.

He lives alone in the house where he was born, on the outskirts of the village. Neither wife nor child is in the vicinity – although in his younger days he was apparently such a potent stud that he begat three children with three different women. They all live in other parts of the country. '*Bof*,' says Jean-Pierre, '*c'est la vie.*' His next child will grow up near him. And then he smiles expectantly, as if he's hoping that you'll volunteer to be the next child's mother.

Some of the village gossips dismiss Madame Voisine's bedridden husband's mysterious illness as incurable laziness, but Madame Voisine never tires of sharing the latest, gruesome symptoms with her neighbours. Last night again, the most terrible stabbing pains way down in the lower body. Didn't sleep a wink. *Quelle horreur!* Is it any wonder she looks like a washed-out dishtowel this morning?

Now you have to smile because, no matter how she suffers, Madame Voisine could never look remotely washed out. Not with those shiny black eyes reminding you of a mischievous little bird. Not with that tiny beak that's always painted red. Above all, not with hair the colour of a slice of melon.

When it's your turn to pay at last, you too have to exchange a few words with the owner. 'Bonjour, madame. Ça va? Et les petits-enfants?' And as you leave the shop with your purchases, don't ever forget to greet everyone in the queue behind you. 'Au revoir, m'ssieurs-dames.'

It can be a convivial business, this waiting in line at the store counter. For the price of an apple and six eggs, you also get the latest village gossip. That's how I think of it these days at any rate.

In my first year I saw this ritual as a total waste of time. I'd dash into the shop because I needed milk or cheese, and not because I wanted to listen to the haemorrhoid problems of complete strangers. Every time I had to wait in line, in a shop, a bank or a post office, my blood started to boil. And then I went back to South Africa for a visit and before I knew it, I was greeting the cashier at the Seven Eleven like an old friend. She barely glanced up from the buttons on her cash register. After I'd paid I said a friendly good-bye, the way I'd been taught in the French country-side. The cashier didn't even hear me. She was already busy with the next customer.

Then it struck me. I'd grown used to the leisurely, social way of doing things. I'd even learnt to like it.

Ever since then I've tried to control my impatience. These days I know that every time I need a loaf of bread or postage stamps or a new cheque book, I'm embarking on a ritual that could take at least a quarter of an hour. And why not? The day has hours enough if you live around here.

But there are still times when the leisurely pace gets me down. Like when I need a plumber urgently because the geyser in the bathroom has packed up and, after two days of cold showers in the middle of winter, I finally find one who answers his phone only to tell me to expect him in three months' time. Then I want to smash that plumber's head with his own pliers and go back to live in the city.

And of course if, after another two days of desperate phone calls, you do find a plumber who promises to come around in a day or two, then you might as well realise that he is having you on. It's not that all plumbers are lazy or liars. It's just that they, along with pretty much everyone who lives here, have an incredibly vague concept of time.

When I was small, my mother did her best to find a compromise between the theory of evolution and the Bible story about the Earth being created in seven days. A biblical day, she explained to me, could mean a million years. Rather a difficult concept for a child – but now that I live here, I understand that story much better. A Provençal day may not be quite the same as a million years, but it never means literally one day. It can take a few days, weeks, even months (of cold showers), before the plumber finally arrives.

I have nothing against plumbers. The bureaucrats of this region have the same vague concept of time – but you've already heard me fume about that elsewhere. Even bankers transact their business at a snail's pace. When we wanted to buy our stone house opposite the abbey, it was touch and go whether the transaction would go through because it took our banker three weeks to mail an urgent document to a bigger branch in a neighbouring village.

The document would've arrived there sooner if we'd offered to deliver it on foot.

Meanwhile I was literally losing my hair because of the stress. The bank manager, I thought, was stalling on purpose. Playing for time, I thought, because he was understandably reluctant to grant a home loan to an *étrangère* without a steady income. A foreigner who claimed she was a writer in a language he'd never heard of.

Alain tried to console me, as always. Nothing happens quickly in this part of the world – surely I should know that by now? I would not be consoled and pulled another tuft of hair out of my head. We were talking about an important transaction, I moaned.

Surely buying a house was not the same as buying a loaf of bread!

I'd expected to wait at most three weeks to hear whether the home loan had been granted. In the end it took almost three months. I was almost bald by the time the banker called us with the happy news.

But now I know. In this region, buying a house is indeed a time-consuming business. Actually quite a lot like buying an unusually large loaf of bread.

In January, when the naked plane trees and poplars stand shivering in the wind, you can buy a beautiful tart from your local baker with a lucky charm of plastic or porcelain hidden inside it. Along with the tart the baker will give you a crown made of gold cardboard. Back home, with a fire burning in the hearth, the tart is cut and the slices shared out among the company. If you find the lucky charm in your slice, you get to wear the golden crown and become king for a day.

That's how it's supposed to work anyway. I've heard of more than one greedy tart eater who accidentally swallowed the lucky charm.

But that's probably also part of this tradition – the first of many that are spread like lucky charms throughout every French year. Some of these traditions are so old that no one can really tell you how they came about. Early in February, for example, in every house in every street, pancakes are baked for the feast of *Chandeleur*. Literally translated, it means the feast of candles, the English Candlemas, a Roman Catholic celebration that commemorates the purification of the Virgin Mary. Whatever *that* may mean. This bit of information I had to look up in a book because none of my neighbours could offer an explanation.

Not even our local historian. Although Jean-Pierre will concede that he's not an expert in the sphere of Catholic habits. Like most of the villagers he'll one day be buried by the Catholic Church, but while he lives he stays as far as possible away from any church.

And what on earth could the connection be between candles and pancakes? Another thing no one can explain. *C'est comme ça*, says Jean-Pierre, with one of those infuriating Gallic shrugs. That's just the way it is. Tradition is tradition, he mutters and raises his glass to his lips. The reasons don't really matter.

The tart with the lucky charm and the crown, I've learnt by now, has to do with the Three Wise Men, or the Three Kings, as they're called around here. The Catholic feast of *Épiphanie* is celebrated early in January, but this royal tart is eaten everywhere throughout the first month of the year. When my son has his birthday at the end of January, he takes three tarts with three crowns to school to share with his classmates. For the past couple of years he's insisted on Harry Potter tarts.

Yes, like all really ancient traditions, this one also has to be adapted from time to time to appeal to the younger generation. The newest fad is tarts with Harry Potter lucky charms instead of the traditional figures from the stable in Bethlehem. Three Magicians tarts you might say, instead of Three Kings tarts. So far the cardboard crown hasn't been replaced with a collapsible witch's hat. But it may just be a matter of time.

The ritual around the dividing of the tart, however, remains inviolate. To ensure scrupulous fairness, the tart is placed on a table and the youngest child in the company crawls underneath the table. The person who cuts the tart has to ask the child under the table who each slice is for.

Of course you can do it without all the fuss. Simply serve a slice of tart on a plate for each person. But then you turn a magical moment into an ordinary one.

And that would be such a shame.

We need magical moments. We need crowns and carnivals and candle flames on cakes to lend excitement and magic to our everyday existence. We need rituals and traditions.

Since coming to live here, in an ancient part of the world rich in ancient traditions, I've learnt that tradition can comfort like nothing else. Except perhaps good chocolate.

By the middle of February, when the almond blossoms appear like gauzy white brides in the frozen landscape, it's carnival time. Another Catholic tradition. *Mardi Gras* literally means 'Fat Tuesday', a day of feasting at the start of a religious fast. But like so many church traditions, this one too is based on a much older heathen habit. Long before the church became a part of Europeans' lives, long before February was called February, the end of the European winter was already marked by a joyous feast.

For centuries the radiant almond blossoms have been the first signs of mercy, an annual miracle heralding warmer weather, proof of new life deep beneath the frozen earth.

And as happens with these traditions, the carnival in the French *campagne* has also become a hodgepodge of ecclesiastical and older customs. In our village, as in most of the other villages around here, every year a life-sized straw doll is made and then mercilessly condemned to death. No one ever has the chance to state the accused's side of the story. The sentence is always the same: the sinner must be burnt at the stake. In the presence of a crowd of villagers, the straw doll – which here is called *Carmentran*, but elsewhere by other names – is doused with fuel and devoured by flames.

Not exactly what you'd call a fair hearing, eh?

The first time I watched this grotesque spectacle, surrounded by jesting children dressed up as devils and skeletons, laughing mothers dressed up as witches, unrecognisable fathers with wigs on their heads and make-up on their faces, my stomach somersaulted with shock. For my merry French neighbours it was just another one of the many ancient rituals to which they've been exposed since childhood. For me, fresh from a country where until fairly recently people were sentenced in the same way by township crowds, doused with petrol and burnt alive, it was something completely different.

It's the winter that is being metaphorically burnt, Alain explained when he read the discomfort in my eyes. The cold and dark being driven away by heat and light. And then there is of course the symbolic meaning of the straw. The doll is made from straw – the food that keeps farm animals alive during the long winter – to show that very soon the straw won't be needed any more, that the animals will be able to graze outside again.

Oui, oui, oui, I murmured. If you look at it in that light, it's probably just innocent fun. But it's taught me that not all traditions offer comfort.

A tradition you don't know can be a terrifying experience.

Because France is France, food is usually part of every tradition. The Three Kings tart in January, pancake in February, chocolate eggs in March and April. And we're not talking about the mass-produced eggs that these days you find all over the world. We're talking about *oeuvres d'art* exhibited in the display windows of *chocolatiers* and *pâtisseries*, as magnificent (and sometimes almost as expensive) as Fabergé eggs. Easter eggs made from real chocolate (and by real chocolate we mean chocolate that contains at least 70 per cent cocoa) and decorated with colourful chicks and flowers made from glazed sugar or marzipan. At Easter the art of the *chocolatier* reaches its annual climax.

I've never yet had the courage to put one of these artistic eggs into my mouth. (Of course the fact that I've never had the money to buy one of these artistic eggs has made this easier.) And for the children an Easter egg is an Easter egg – of which you try to eat the greatest possible number in the shortest possible time – therefore we buy them the cheapest ones we can find.

For some food traditions you don't even need a feast day. Once you've bought the spring's first bunch of dark green asparagus at a Provençal market, an ordinary day has turned into a feast day anyway. The mere thought that tonight you will eat six steamed asparagus with a little mayonnaise is enough to make the sun shine brighter, make the baker's surly wife seem friendlier, make your children's whining sound like music. Well, almost.

A month or so later you pick the first black-red cherries of summer in an orchard on a hill, and the miracle repeats itself. An ordinary day becomes extraordinary. ('Little pigeon hearts', these cherries are called in French, and I could swear their poetic name makes them taste even better.) It's the same with the first bowl of seductive strawberries, the first melons as firm as a young man's bottom, the first sour-sweet and sensual apricots of the summer. The ancient tradition of fresh food, the right product in the right season, a pleasure that globalisation and mass distribution and deep freezes and microwave ovens have so far failed to efface. That's what we're talking about here.

On the first day of May you celebrate the arrival of spring by giving a plant to someone you love. Not just any old plant of course. Tradition dictates that it must be a *muguet*, the shy, small lily of the valley that is sold on every street corner on this day. For the rest of the day you can do as you like, as it's a public holiday, but France being France, the rest of the day usually includes a feast. Preferably in the open air.

On my first French May Day, one of my neighbours invited me to such an open-air meal at a nearby picnic place. Because May Day is also known as Workers' Day, it remains a highlight on the calendar for the Communist Party. And given that the local branch of the Communist Party had arranged this meal, I wasn't exactly expecting a culinary climax. More like a sandwich on a paper plate, a paper cup of cheap red wine and perhaps a few revolutionary slogans into the bargain.

How wrong I was.

The scene took my breath away. And that was before I'd tasted the food. I felt as if I'd fallen into a Fellini film. Long tables with white tablecloths were spread in the shade of plane trees, with plates of porcelain and glasses of glass, many bottles of fine wine and a fantastic four-course meal that lasted for hours.

In this country even the Communists are hedonists, I discovered that day. Stylish gourmets. Lovers of good wine.

This was a country where I could live, I decided that day.

Once summer is in full bloom, along with the roses and lavender,
holidaymakers converge on the sunny south – an annual migra-
tion that has become a tradition in itself – and every village looks
for an excuse to hold a festival. Most villages already have a *fête
votive*, something like a birthday that is celebrated every year, but
it simply isn't enough. In summer every village also has a wine
festival or a flower festival or a music festival or a book festival.
There is always an excuse for another festival.

Nearby, for example, there is a village called Mondragon that
was plagued by a cruel dragon many centuries ago. Don't laugh.
It is true. Well, if you've ever been at Mondragon's annual
Festival of the Dragon on a warm moonlit evening, you'd also
want to believe that it was true. The villagers, young and old,
wear medieval costumes – noblewomen and knights on horse-
back, dignified monks and screaming witches, artisans and acro-
bats – and enact the legend of the dragon in the open air. The
story tells how one after the other brave knights came to fight the
dragon until at last one of them broke the monster's power, and
married a beautiful local princess as his reward.

The dragon is a grotesque mechanical monster, but the story is
enacted by real people and animals. You see the knights' armour
shine in the moonlight, you hear the clanging of their swords and
the nervous snorting of the horses, and it all seems so real that it's
easy to be carried away. Children adore the spectacle – but even
cynical grown-ups manage to believe in fairytales for one night.

On July 14 the summer's festivities reach a countrywide climax with the *Fête Nationale*, which commemorates the fall of the
notorious Bastille prison in 1789. In Paris there is usually a
breathtaking fireworks display at the Eiffel Tower. In our modest
village the show is more modest – just a few crackers, really, let
off near the municipal garbage cans – but for the villagers who

gather on the bridge over the river to admire the colours and sounds against the night sky, it's another tradition that they won't miss for anything.

Last year, even Jean-Pierre dragged himself away from the bar to stand on the bridge accompanied by an excited niece. The show doesn't start until midnight, by which time Jean-Pierre is usually far from sober. Perhaps his inebriated state made him see double, two crackers for every one that was let off. Perhaps that made everything somehow more spectacular. When all was over – and it was over very soon – he gave a deep sigh, wiped his cheek and declared: '*Bof*. Now I can die happy.'

Irony? With a character like Jean-Pierre you never know.

After the fireworks there is drinking and dancing all night long under the plane trees on the town square.

Every such rural feast makes me realise once again that the countryside is really the same wherever you are in the Western world. Okay, in South Africa we don't often eat outside at long tables. It's more a case of men gathering around the braai fire and women trying to balance paper plates on their laps, and in South Africa you get just one plate loaded with meat instead of a succession of several dishes. And of course the language sounds different. But these are minor differences.

What strikes me every time is that the people behave in exactly the same way. The false bravado of the men, the chattering of the women, the teenagers who slink off to smoke in dark corners, the younger children dancing with each another and the toddlers falling asleep underneath the tables. Where I live now the people even look like my aunts and uncles in the South African countryside. Jean-Pierre's bushy moustache might be typically French, but with his bulky body and paunch you'd struggle to pick him out from among the farmers of Porterville or Piketberg.

It's different in Northern Europe. Dutch and Irish farmers don't look like Afrikaner farmers. They're too pale, their cheeks too rosy, their way of dress determined by rain and mud and snow. And American farmers, as everyone knows, wear straw hats and denim dungarees. But the farmers and the workers of Provence wear khaki shorts or old jeans and short-sleeved shirts, their faces are bronzed by the sun and on the rest of their bodies they sport that famous Boere tan that's so conspicuous on South African beaches. Pale chest, upper arms and thighs, dark brown forearms, knees and calves.

Perhaps it's not just the sun and the clothing that make them look so familiar. Perhaps the genes of the French Huguenots are still abundantly present in the bodies of rural Afrikaners.

Or maybe it's just a resemblance imagined by a lapsed boere-meisie to make her feel a little more at home in the French *campagne*.

Later in the year there are other, quieter joys. After the first rains of autumn, you can hunt for wild mushrooms under damp leaves in the nearest forest. Not that my Frenchman and I ever find many mushrooms. We were both raised in the city. We lack the patient eye and leisurely pace of the seasoned mushroom hunter. What we have found instead of mushrooms are friends who know how to find mushrooms.

Not a bad arrangement, I assure you.

At the end of October, when the vineyards start to lose their gold and orange glow, we celebrate *Toussaint*. All Saints' Day on 1 November remains a religious feast day, but in recent years the American Hallowe'en has also caught on here. Children dress up in gory costumes (Daniel usually wears the same costume as for the carnival in February), shopkeepers decorate their display windows with spider webs and pumpkins, and in our neighbouring village they sell pumpkin soup, pumpkin tart, pumpkin pie and other pumpkin dishes on the market square overlooked by a medieval castle. It's a bit silly, because France isn't a pumpkin country, but there you are. Even the oldest European traditions have little chance against blatant American commercialism.

By late autumn, just before the winter really starts to bite, the first wines of the recent harvest are blessed by the priest and tasted by the entire community. In Tulette, a neighbouring village that Daniel initially called Toilet, historical costumes are worn to celebrate this festival. Enormous barrels of wine are loaded onto horse carts that are drawn through the town in a demure procession and parked on the market square. For the rest of the day you wander from barrel to barrel with a glass in your hand to taste and decide which cellar, in your modest opinion, has fared the best this year. The later, the merrier – and the colder. After dark you push your way into a warm spot close to an enormous fire to chew on roasted chestnuts and sip hot spicy wine to thaw out your body before you start on the journey home.

And then, before you know it, it's December and Christmas is on its way. Yes, around here Christmas always takes you a little by surprise, unlike South Africa where some stores start to advertise the festive season as early as October. Over here, in October the shop windows are still decorated with pumpkins for *Toussaint*. And in November, with vine branches for the festival of the new wine. We're well into December before the Christmas decorations are brought out and the Christmas lights switched on in the streets.

And to me it seems that's how it should be. There's a time for every tradition – and October is simply too early to start celebrating Christmas.

I've never experienced the proverbial White Christmas in Provence. A White Boxing Day, yes, as well as a White New Year, a White Week in November and several White Days in February. Snow is not, unfortunately, delivered on demand. Usually, Christmas Day is just bitterly cold, without the glamour of snow. The trees spread their bare branches against the blue sky, and the stone buildings, having lost their summery covering of creepers, look a little embarrassed at being caught naked in public, especially on Christmas Day. And the mistral blows as only the mistral can.

The biggest advantage of a cold Christmas, even if it isn't a white one, is that you can eat so much more than when you're celebrating a warm one. And this is an enormous advantage in the land of gourmands and *grande cuisine*. I'd always thought that my Afrikaner family was scandalously extravagant when it came to food for the Christmas table. Until I saw Alain's French family's table on Christmas Day.

Actually the French celebrate an entire week of *gourmandise*. They start eating on Christmas Eve and don't stop until New Year's Day. They spend a lot of time complaining that they cannot possibly manage another bite – before opening their mouths again for the next irresistible treat. It always makes me think of a silly Afrikaans nursery rhyme: 'She says she isn't hungry, but goodness, can she eat.' Oysters and *coquilles St Jacques* and other treasures from the sea, *pâté de foie gras* and truffles, duck and ham and red meat, a variety of cheeses that you'll be dreaming about for the rest of the year, chocolate and glazed-fruit sweets and ice-cream cakes. All washed down of course with the best wines in the world, champagne from Champagne, cognac from Cognac.

And then the second day of January arrives and you make up your mind to fast for a week. But then you walk past a bakery and you see the seductive Three Kings tarts in the display window. And suddenly you remember, oh yes, it's *that* time of the year again.

And then you buy the tart with the cardboard crown because you can't disappoint the children, can you? And then you join the children in eating the tart because what else can you do? Tradition is tradition, isn't it?

Long live tradition!

12 On a high note

Some of the inhabitants of our region prefer to flee during summer, doesn't really matter where, just to get away from the swarms of holidaymakers, the traffic jams, the uninvited guests. It's an understandable impulse, which our family has also occasionally obeyed, but not one that I'd recommend without reserve. It's true that sometimes there are so many Germans, Americans, Britons and Dutch at Vaison-la-Romaine's morning market that you start to wonder if you're still in France. But here in the south summer still brings more pleasure than pain.

That's how I feel at the moment at any rate. We'll talk again in a couple of years.

Among the greatest joys of the southern summer are the music festivals held in the ancient Roman amphitheatres. Opera in Orange, jazz in Vienne, modern dance in Vaison-la-Romaine, always under the stars, on stages that were built more than two thousand years ago, applauded by audiences on uncomfortable stone benches.

A performance by an international diva like Angela Gheorghiu and her husband Roberto Alagna, in the romantic title roles of Gounod's opera *Roméo et Juliette*, would be remarkable in any circumstances. In the ancient theatre of Orange, on a windless moonlit night, it becomes one of those now-I-can-die-happy experiences. That, at any rate, was what I wrote to my friends the next day and, unlike Jean-Pierre after the modest fireworks display in our village, I wasn't being ironic.

For such a world-class spectacle you pay the sort of money that could've bought each of your four children a new pair of shoes. Even if you book almost a year in advance, as we did; even if you choose the cheapest seats, as we did, so high up in the theatre that leaning forward makes your head swim, it remains an almost illicit luxury. On the other hand, if we'd had more money, we would probably also have been more blasé about such unique experiences. Now we enjoy every musical outing, every summer, as if it's our first and our last.

Fortunately there is also live music that doesn't cost a *centime*. (And I'm not talking about Alain and his musical pals' weekly practice session in the courtyard.) The nearby town of Bollène presents a week-long festival of free street music every summer. Every evening, on the square outside the stately old town hall, different groups entertain a crowd of people of all ages. This year the emphasis was on gypsy music, mostly of such a high standard that you couldn't believe it was free.

On the other hand, last summer our family also attended a free 'musical performance' on the sports ground of Tulette, also known as Toilet, which was such an incredible concoction of kitsch costumes, unimaginative dance routines and forgettable music that only Mia, then two years old, could get any enjoyment from it. *Ze Beautiful Show*, this spectacle was called. Perhaps the silly French-English title should have warned us. But it was free and we had nothing better to do. Or so we thought. After half an hour spent watching a dozen dancers in lots of feathers and very little clothes – but not so little as to titillate any of the boys in our company – and a few mediocre singers who turned songs from well-known American musicals into unrecognisable French gibberish, we decided that watching even the most boring TV series at home would be more exciting.

But, to each his own. The next day Madame Voisine told everyone in the queue at the supermarket that for her it had been *une soirée inoubliable*. When she asked what I'd thought of it, I couldn't bear to dampen her childlike enthusiasm. (With her bedridden husband, any evening away from home was probably unforgettable.) So I just said hmmm, for me too it had been 'an unforgettable evening'. Though not, of course, for the same reasons.

A much pleasanter experience is the *Fête de Musique*, which is celebrated every year on June 21, all over the country, from the biggest cities to the tiniest hamlets, to make the shortest night of the year even shorter. There are voices singing, drums ruffling and trumpets groaning under plane trees on every town square, in parks and cafés, on sidewalks and street corners. Every kind of music is performed, from baroque to rock, on every kind of instrument from traditional Provençal flutes to booming electric guitars.

This year, for example, two of the children and I hit the road to Vaison-la-Romaine on the evening of June 21. In our own village there was just one little amateur orchestra on the square a few steps away from our living-room window, and after three lacklustre *chansons* we all fled from the living room. But that's what makes the music festival so much fun. If you don't like what you're hearing in one village, you simply go to the next one. Which is never more than three kilometres away.

The next day Jean-Pierre declared that the music hadn't been up to much, *pas terrible*, but the singer had been something for a tired man's eyes. And as always when he sees a beautiful woman or even just thinks of a beautiful woman, his dark eyes shone brighter than usual. But even if the singer had been ugly as sin, Jean-Pierre wouldn't have driven to the next village. He'd 'attended' the musical performance sitting on his barstool like every other evening. I sometimes envy Jean-Pierre's complete satisfaction with his environment, his utter lack of curiosity about the rest of the world, his unshakeable certainty that he knows every-thing that is worth knowing about everything around him.

Jean-Pierre knows where he belongs. In this village, in this bar, on this chair. He'll never know what it's like to be an *étranger*.

In Vaison-la-Romaine, barely twenty minutes' drive from where we live, all three of us – Daniel, Mia and I – found happi-ness. Not all of us at the same time, unfortunately. But we try hard to be a democratic family.

First there was a group of high-school students who bombard-ed the sedate crowd at open-air cafés with furious rock. The androgynous singer screamed out the lyrics of Nirvana and Marilyn Manson in a hoarse voice while a few dozen of his (her?) fellow students danced near the small stage. At least I think they were dancing. They seemed to be trying to knock each other down by leaping against each other with their full weight. My three-year-old daughter, who in normal circumstances adores dancing, hid in my lap, terrified. My eleven-year-old son thought the group was really cool. For him they were the highlight of this year's music festival.

I found the high-school rockers a bit silly, but certainly not boring. The next group, middle-aged and balding, entertained the crowd with pop hits from the sixties and seventies. For me this performance was plain boring. But Mia immediately jumped from my lap to dance with the other pre-school children in the street, and protested loudly when I dragged her away.

A few streets on I finally found my bit of happiness. A group of youthful musicians playing some jolly jazz. Ridiculous outfits, broad grins, lots of wind instruments. I protested loudly when my children dragged me away.

But we drove home satisfied. Each of us had found something to smile about.

Alain's music group were performing in another nearby village that evening. (And just in case you get the impression that I don't support my husband's musical performances, please keep in mind that I listen to their practice sessions every week.) On the way home from Vaison-la-Romaine I stopped at Mondragon to ask how their performance had gone over. (Yes, the village tormented by the legendary dragon.) Alas, nothing was over yet. It was way past midnight and most of the audience had gone to bed, but a few amateur groups were enthusiastically entertaining each another.

I listened while a bearded, hairy, tattooed truck driver mutilated Bob Dylan's *Knockin' on Heaven's Door.* Not only was his French accent as thick as butter, but his voice was atrocious. I decided to go to bed too. Alain and his colleagues carried on making music until sunrise.

There's just one night in the year when a French truck driver can imagine he's Bob Dylan, when a high-school student can believe he or she has turned into Marilyn Manson, and when my own better half can pretend he's Jacques Brel. Just as well it's the shortest night of the year.

The previous year's *Fête de Musique* was the historic occasion of Sesame's first public performance. After more than a year of rehearsals, Alain and his colleagues took on the public – on a small stretch of sidewalk in a back alley of Avignon. Well, the Beatles started in an obscure beer cellar in Germany. Everyone has to start somewhere.

Not expecting them to draw many spectators, I commandeered everyone in the house to go and cheer them on. Fortunately it was summer and the house, as in every summer, was chock-a-block. Besides me and the four children, there was the ever-present Nephew from the North; Daniel's friend from Stellenbosch, Josua, who was staying with us while his mother was on a walking pilgrimage; my dad who'd come to help us with improvements to the house; and a few other lost souls. Along with the other Sesame members' companions, children, stepchildren and children-in-law, we formed a small crowd. Small but loud. The street echoed with our enthusiastic applause.

For my dad, who barely understood a word of French, it must have been hard to respond enthusiastically to a lot of unfamiliar *chansons* whose lyrics are usually more interesting than the tunes. I bought him a few beers and told him to imagine he was at Newlands. (Cheer like you would every time Western Province scored a try.) It worked.

There were even a few *bona fide* spectators who stopped to listen, who laughed in the right places, applauded at the right moments.

A promising start, wasn't it?

That's why a year later I didn't think they'd need my condescending nepotism. This year's musical festival they braved on their own. In a few years, who knows, they might even get paid to perform.

But until then I'll have to keep writing my stories to the beat of the weekly rehearsals in our courtyard.

13 Do it yourself

I'm a spoilt white woman from Africa. There is no way I can deny it. I've always known that I had a privileged childhood purely because I was born in a certain country at a certain time. But exactly how spoilt I was, I realised only here in Europe.

Like most white children in my native land I was surrounded from infancy by almost invisible black angels who did things for me. My bed was made for me, my room tidied for me. When I began to earn my own meagre wage, I employed a black angel of my own (at an even more meagre wage) to wash and iron my clothes once a week. When I went to buy groceries at a supermarket, someone packed my milk and bread and eggs into a plastic bag for me. Or pushed my trolley to my car for me. And when my car needed petrol, then of course someone filled it up for me. While I of course sat lazily behind the steering wheel.

Imagine my shock when I realised that in France I had to fill up my own car. I had no idea how the whole thing worked. I'd never held one of those slack rubber hoses in my life. I hardly knew how to unlock my car's petrol tank.

But I learnt.

I've also learnt how to check my car's oil. (Before, I didn't even know which end of the stick I was supposed to look at when it was held under my nose.) I've even learnt to pack my own groceries with my own hands, in plastic bags I carry with me from supermarket to supermarket – something that is also done in South Africa these days, hip hip hooray.

The hardest thing of all was learning to do my own ironing. Just ask any spoilt woman from Africa what she misses most in Europe. Like me, she will probably spin you a story about dear friends and beloved mountains. But what she misses the most, believe me, is a domestic worker.

Of course it's not politically correct to admit it. My French husband, who was raised in a communist–socialist household, still gets embarrassed every time he has to admit to a friend that his spoilt foreign wife pays someone once a week to help her for a scant hour or two to combat the eternal chaos of a house with six bedrooms.

As far as the rest of the week goes, well, I've just had to learn to live with dust.

Not that I've ever been terribly tidy. I've always believed that life is too short to reorganise your kitchen cupboards once a week or arrange your underwear in a drawer, military-style. Put another way, I'd rather read a book. Or write a book.

But in South Africa I could pay someone to create the illusion of tidiness around me. Put another way, in South Africa I had the luxury of a tidy home without having to lift a finger to keep it tidy. Like all of us spoilt white women from Africa.

Here in Europe I quickly realised that I was faced with a cruel choice. If I wanted my house to be as tidy as the houses I was used to, I'd never read another book. Let alone write one.

In South Africa, I had one child, a cramped cottage and a domestic worker five days a week. Here I have four children, plus the imaginary Heloïse, plus the Nephew from the North, plus a varying collection of all four children's friends, as well as French and South African relatives and friends who regularly come to stay, a sprawling house with half a dozen bedrooms (the last time we counted), and no domestic help.

There was only one solution. Standards would have to drop.

I've learnt to look past spider webs in high corners and dust underneath beds. I've learnt to wear unironed clothes and sleep on creased pillowcases. I've learnt to ignore sticky patches on the fridge and sweet papers on the floor in the boys' bedrooms.

It's a question of survival.

Actually, it's only when South African friends or female relatives come to visit that I suddenly see my environment through my previous, spoilt South African eyes. And then I see everything that I've learnt not to see. And then I shudder.

And yet I've discovered to my surprise that one can live quite comfortably with dust and creases. As far as I know, no one's ever died from sleeping between unironed sheets. Of course it's important to distinguish between harmless chaos on the one hand and unhygienic conditions on the other. Our clothes are seldom ironed but they're washed very regularly. Like our dishes and our bodies.

By the way, I sometimes wonder where the idea comes from that the French don't like to bath. The three Frenchmen in my house – and my half-French daughter – would bath three times a day if I let them. The only family member who ever complains about bath time is Daniel. I attribute it to his African genes. Water is scarce where he comes from.

To survive here, I've therefore learnt to negotiate that fine line between clean dirt, as my mother put it, and dirty dirt. It's a daily rope dance that a circus performer would envy. If I spend too much time doing the housework, there's too little time left for living. If I spend too little time on housework, the chaos gets out of hand and living becomes impossible anyway – for us spoilt brats from Africa, I mean.

I've learnt balance and compromise. I've even learnt to like spiders. (Leave them in their dusty corners. They catch flies and other nasty bugs.) If I think of everything I've learnt to do in the past few years – not because I wanted to but because I had to – sometimes my jaw drops with amazement, as if I were looking at someone else's life. A woman who has mastered the dark secrets of petrol pumps and rusk recipes. A woman who prunes rose trees and fertilises garden soil, sands down door and window frames, hangs wallpaper and paints ceilings and varnishes floors. A women who will even, when absolutely necessary, manage to knock together her own bookcases.

These are all tasks that I would previously have entrusted to someone else without any qualms – a willing family member or a skilled artisan. The latter for a fee of course. Here I have no family members handy. And where artisans are concerned: (a) they're terribly difficult to find; (b) if you're lucky enough to track one down, it's even more difficult to explain to him, in French, what you want him to do; and (c) their fees are usually unaffordable. Therefore I mostly do it myself. With the help of my better half, who is also not exactly gifted when it comes to manual work.

The most elaborate of all the thankless tasks I've learnt to do has to be moving house myself. Moving with bag and baggage from one house to the next. Not once, but three times in as many years.

Let me explain, because I know it sounds too stupid to be true.

I moved to the French countryside because I'd fallen madly in love with a Frenchman. But because we'd both been married before, and were already burdened with children and pets and lots of other baggage, literal and figurative, we thought it would be irresponsible to put all our eggs in one basket from the word go. Put another way, we were at an age when quite a few of our eggs were already broken. And then you don't want to take chances with the remaining eggs.

My son and I therefore didn't move in with Alain and his two sons right away. I rented another house in another village. In other words, we ran separate households. In theory, anyway. In practice we spent most of our time together, either at my house or at his, while the other house stood empty. No. In practice we spent most of our time in a car, en route from one house to the other. And spent most of our money on petrol.

It was the children who after just a few months insisted that we stop the ridiculous driving around and all start living together in one house. So I gave up my rented house and moved into Alain's slightly bigger rented house, while together we looked for an even bigger house. Because by then Mia was already on the way, and no matter how we figured and rearranged the furniture, we just didn't have enough sleeping-place for all our children. Not to mention all our guests.

When at last, after about two years of looking, we found a house with enough rooms – at a price we could more or less afford – I had to move again. I'd thought that the first two moves were difficult, but the third one was in a class by itself.

With the first move I paid a company in South Africa to pack all my possessions into boxes and load them onto a ship. It was just the unpacking on this side of the ocean I had to handle myself. With the second move barely a few months later, I couldn't afford a second round of professional help. I was still busy paying for the first one.

It was therefore a case of do it yourself. Pack your things yourself. And rent a vehicle yourself and hoist the enormous double bed out of the first-floor bedroom window yourself because the staircase is too narrow and there isn't any other way to get the bed out of the house. A few of Alain's friends came to lend a hand with muscles and ropes, but the double bed was permanently damaged nonetheless. I opted not to complain, because at one point it looked as if the bed was going to fall on the helpers' heads in the street below and then the damage would've been quite a lot worse. To the helpers, if not to the bed.

The third move was much more complicated. Some of the furniture, kitchenware and bed linen in our rented home belonged to the owner of the house. Some of the furniture, books and ornaments belonged to Alain's former wife. Then there were Alain's possessions. And my own, of course. All mixed up together. Most of my own things I could recognise, but every time I wanted to pack a plate or a book that didn't belong to me into a box, I had to ask Alain who was the rightful owner – to make sure I wasn't carrying off the landlord's or the ex's things.

It took weeks to get everything packed.

The last week before the official moving day Alain started to cart the boxes, smaller pieces of furniture, the paintings and suitcases and so on to the new house. Fortunately, the new house was less than ten kilometres away from the old one. That meant we could move bit by bit. Every morning on his way to work, Alain first went to unpack his overloaded car at the new house. During the day I diligently filled more boxes and wrapped fragile possessions in newspaper. In the evening when Alain got home, the full boxes were once again stacked up to the ceiling. Then we moved a few more loads until our muscles ached and we were too tired to even pick up a pot plant. And the next day the packing and carting would start all over again ...

Until D-Day. D for *déménager*, the French word for moving house, the day on which we could take occupation of our new house. Which, as the result of unusually bad planning and a lack of vision, happened to be the first of May. Workers' Day. The one day in other words when not a single worker in France is prepared to work. Even if we could have afforded a team of labourers (we couldn't, just to be absolutely clear), they would've declined our offer in order to go on a picnic with their comrades instead. I would too, if I were them. The memory of my first magnificent 'communist' picnic was still fresh in my mind.

We could also not, as with the previous move, count on friends to help because on this particular Workers' Day the entire France was in a state of shock. Or that part of France that we counted among our friends. A week earlier, Jean-Marie le Pen of the far-right *Front National* had quite unexpectedly become Jacques Chirac's only official opponent in the upcoming presidential election. As a result, this public holiday was one of countrywide mobilisation, of protests and marches, of banners and slogans. The country of *liberté, égalité et fraternité* was facing oppression, racism and hatred between brothers. Everyone we knew, everyone we might have asked to help with our move, wanted to take part in the protest.

So did Alain, of course.

So did I. Or rather, on any other day of the year I would've called out: 'So do I!' But on this day we'd borrowed our Italian neighbour's truck to transport the washing machine, the tumble dryer, beds and wardrobes and other massive pieces of furniture to our new house. By sunset the old house had to be empty and the new one habitable. I expected the French nation to understand that in circumstances such as these, protesting was out of the question. That I had to choose between the political and the personal. And that, with a heavy conscience, I chose the personal.

Put it this way. The fridge in the old house was full of food that had to be moved to the new house before the power in the old house was cut. Surely I couldn't stand in the street shouting slogans while the food lay rotting in the fridge!

Well, the French nation might have understood – after all, food has an inviolable status in this country – but my French husband refused to see my point. It was our duty to join the protest, he declared. The whole lot of us. *En famille.* He'd always regretted that he was too young to take part in the student protests of May 1968 in Paris. He could never forgive himself if he also missed the protests of May 2002.

And just to make sure that I understood the gravity of the matter, he began to sing the stirring French anthem at the top of his voice: *Allons, enfants de la patrieee ...*

I had a vision of how his ancestors must have looked in the moments before they chopped off Marie Antoinette's head. I decided not to argue anymore.

The food rotted while we marched in Bollène.

It wasn't a particularly glorious march. Just a modest country version of the inflamed crowds who gathered on Bastille Square in Paris that day. But Mia sat on her father's shoulders and grabbed the *tricouleur* out of someone's hand and waved it around enthusiastically. We have a potential agitator in our midst, I thought while I watched her. A leader in the student protests of May 2020.

I did my best not to think of the rotten food in the fridge.

Madame Voisine also protested in Bollène that day. She left the ailing Monsieur in the care of an unwilling relative and relived her impetuous youth by walking out in front of the marchers. Her bright orange hairdo led the rest of us like a burning torch. Some things are more important than a sick husband. Or a fridge full of rotten food, I realised a little shamefully.

Even Jean-Pierre took part in the political activity in his own way. By sitting in his usual place in the bar, patiently tasting his *pastis* and speculating about Le Pen's chances against Chirac in the tones of an objective visitor from another planet. Usually he's as determined to avoid any political discussion as he is to avoid any steady work. It causes bad feeling, he believes, particularly in a bar. But on this historic day he made a historic exception.

It was late at night by the time we had finished moving. I swore I would never move again as long as I lived. That's what I say after every move, Alain reminded me.

All right, then. I'll make a more realistic promise. If I ever want to marry again, I decided on the day of my second wedding, it won't be during the grape harvest in the south of France. And if I ever move again, I decided on the night of my third French move, it won't be on Workers' Day.

On all future Workers' Days, I want to do no work, like everyone around me. And hopefully it won't be necessary to protest either. Hopefully, I'll be able to stretch out in the hammock underneath the plane tree and read a book while I gently rock myself to sleep.

And if there's anything that absolutely *has* to be done, then please, please, I don't want to do it myself.

14   Where will my help come from?

So there we were in the stone house in Church Street. A three-storey house with many rooms, two storeys in considerable need of repair but still habitable. And a third storey 'with potential', as the estate agent said. For those of you who don't understand estate agents' euphemisms, this meant that the third storey was a big black hole of chaos. A dark staircase with no ceiling, an enormous attic where a century's dust lay ankle-deep, and two rooms where no one had lived for fifty years. With no lights or wall sockets or any form of electrical wiring, no water supply and no heating.

And the long summer holiday was two months away, when Thomas and the Nephew from the North would arrive, as well as more sleepover guests than in any other summer because of course all Alain's relatives (and there are many) were in a hurry to see our new home. And we didn't have enough room for our own son and his cousin, let alone all the other guests.

In other words we had two months in which to transform the black hole on the top storey into a habitable space.

Do it yourself? No, I've learnt to do many things myself but I've not yet learnt to work a miracle. This task was way beyond my powers. I needed help – urgent, thorough and above all affordable help – and I knew I wasn't going to find it in the French labour market.

Where would my help come from? Where I came from, of course.

I phoned my dad. I offered him a plane ticket, plus all the delicious French food he could eat, plus all the French wine he wanted to drink, plus a chance to see his grandchildren. If he'd just come for a month or so to help with the alterations to our new home.

An offer he couldn't refuse. Not when he heard the despair in his daughter's voice.

My dad is one of those DIY-ers who can turn their hand to anything. He knows how to lay bricks, saw planks and mix concrete, he even knows enough about electrical wiring and plumbing pipes to get by. For the plumbing we employed a French plumber all the same. The pipes look different from those in South Africa and we didn't want to take any chances. The electrical wiring also looks different from that in South Africa, but in this old house the wiring was in such a dubious state that a bit of tinkering couldn't make matters much worse. Later, we decided, we would get a French electrician to rewire the entire house from scratch. Now, however, we had to conjure up two bedrooms and a bathroom before the start of the summer holidays.

Conjure was the operative word.

My dad managed to do in one month what would've taken three French artisans three months.

Jean-Pierre offered to help, not very convincingly, and looked quite relieved when I said thank you, it wouldn't be necessary. When I added that we'd been fortunate to find a muscular young labourer to lend a hand on odd days, he immediately assured me that there was nothing the matter with *his* muscles. Which I don't doubt. With his bulky shoulders he is still as strong as an ox. But an ox who wanted to sit in a bar all day long wouldn't help construction along much.

So Jean-Pierre decided to help us in an advisory if not in a physical capacity. For the entire month he displayed an intense interest in the construction – from the safe distance of his bar stool – and constantly offered his opinion on which was the best paint for damp walls, the best way to install a shower, the best plan for a false ceiling. Without once lifting a finger. Except of course to raise his glass to his lips.

Alain and I helped where we could, with sanding and painting and other 'easier' tasks. But to be honest, I found even the easiest assignments difficult. I'd hoped that my dad's DIY talents would turn out to be hereditary, or at least contagious, but I was deeply disappointed by how helpless my own hands turned out to be.

My most time-consuming and demanding task had, however, nothing to do with my hands. Or rather, my hands were involved in a different way. I had to become a full-time interpreter for my dad who doesn't speak a word of French. This meant that every time he wanted to say something to the muscular labourer or the plumber – who of course spoke nothing but French – I had to be the go-between. And because my French vocabulary was far from being broad enough to include any technical terminology, I had to use my hands. Sign language became my salvation.

Every time my dad needed a tiny screw or a piece of wire or a bag of cement from a hardware store, I had to go along to do the talking. We soon realised that it would be more practical if he stayed at home to carry on with the urgent construction work while I ventured into the hardware stores alone.

I'm not the sort of woman you'd expect to find hanging around hardware stores. Indeed, I was amazed to discover that such women existed. An entire species of which I'd been previously unaware, men and women (mostly men, granted) who spend their time in this peculiar way. Rooting around shelves full of screws and nails, deliberating over tins of paint and bottles filled with chemicals, contemplating the thickness of planks and the cost of tiles per square metre. A whole new universe was unfolding before me.

The next thing I knew, I was all alone in this parallel universe with a piece of plastic tubing and a strange little metal ring clutched in my sweaty palm. My assignment was to buy a few metres of this plastic tubing and a dozen little rings. I didn't have the foggiest idea what these things were used for. I didn't know what they were called. Not even in English or Afrikaans. Now I had to track them down in French.

When at last I left the shop with my purchases, I had to fight the temptation to wave my fist triumphantly in the air. I felt like the mythical Hercules after he got his hands on the golden apples of the Hesperides.

When I got home, my dad took one look at my booty and announced it unsuitable. The plastic tube was a millimetre too thin, he could tell right away. And the metal rings didn't look up to the task. My golden apples turned to dust before my eyes.

Back I went to the parallel universe to keep searching. My dad in the meantime had pressed a strange screw-type object in my hand: 'While you're there, get me ten of these too.'

So it continued, day after miserable day. When Alain came to bed one night and saw that I, instead of reading a novel as usual, was studying a catalogue from a hardware store, he burst out laughing. I didn't even look up. By then my sense of humour had also gone missing somewhere in the parallel universe, along with a growing collection of nameless screws and unmentionable bits of tools.

To summarise. By the end of my dad's stay I was on kissing terms with the staff of several hardware stores in the area. Of course in the French countryside it doesn't take much to get to the kissing stage, but still. I never dreamed when I came to live here that I'd have such regular intimate contact with such a wide variety of do-it-yourself men.

Definitely what the Americans would call a learning curve.

And once you find yourself inside such a curve, it's a little like getting on to a roller-coaster. You build up a kind of momentum. You can't shout that you want to get off halfway. At any rate that is what happened to me. I remain strangely drawn to hardware catalogues to this day.

After my dad left, Alain and I had to do the finishing touches our-selves. Paint more walls, hang more wallpaper, sand and varnish more floors. Replace door handles, put up curtain rails, that sort of thing. Nothing compared to what my dad had accomplished. They were a few insignificant steps for a DIY-er but a giant leap in experience and self-confidence for someone like me.

The result of which was that by the next summer I felt up to saving all the wood on the outside of the house from ruin, single-handed. There were eighteen shutters, numerous window frames, a front door and a massive garage door that had to be sanded, treated and painted from scratch. By single-handed of course I mean Alain's hands and mine. Because what's his is mine, isn't it? Sometimes I battle a little to convince him of that, but in this instance he didn't object too much. We couldn't afford to fly my dad to France again.

We knew it would be a big job – but exactly how big we realised only once we started removing the old layers of paint with a fairly primitive little sanding tool. Apparently it never occurred to any previous owner in the course of a century or so to get rid of the old layers of paint. They just added another coat on top. Or perhaps they started as eagerly as we did, quickly realised how difficult it would be and simply gave up. We refused to give up – we couldn't afford to buy new shutters in a year or two – but we hadn't taken account of fate. Or rather, we hadn't taken account of our fragile, unfit, middle-aged bodies.

Alain's back gave out halfway through. We had to buy painkillers and book a few sessions with a physiotherapist. Then he lay on his back in front of the TV for a week or two, on his doctor's orders, while the true meaning of 'single-handed' finally dawned on me.

I applied several coats of paint to the eight shutters that had already been sanded. A white undercoat first, followed by a 24-hour wait, then a thin first coat of that typically Provençal laven-der blue and another 24-hour wait, then another coat of lavender blue, then wait … After a week my hair, my hands, my feet and especially my nails had acquired an interesting blue sheen. My face began to look like that of someone who was being gently strangled. No matter how vigorously I scrubbed myself in the bath at night, I just couldn't get rid of the blue undertone. And mostly I was too exhausted at night to scrub with any real vigour.

Blue dreams haunted me when I closed my tired eyes at night. Not blue sea or blue sky. Blue paint. I realised for the first time why feeling down is called getting the blues. Rather than getting the reds, let's say, or the greens.

But like all horrible things, this too finally passed. Close to two months later, all the shutters, doors and window frames had at last been painted. Unfortunately, it would take another month to rehang the shutters on the top storey because we didn't have a ladder that was long enough, and because Alain, though he hates to admit it, is terrified of heights. In other words, we were once again at the mercy of a helpful neighbour. In this case one with a long ladder and a head for heights.

In the meantime, the house looked like a senile old woman who, having dressed the bottom half of her body grandly in lavender blue, completely forgot about her naked upper body or her uncombed hair.

And then, when the neighbour finally arrived with his ladder and his head, and every freshly painted shutter was finally in its place, the strangest thing happened.

I'd expected to be so pleased with my husband's and my handiwork that I'd spend hours on the abbey steps across the road admiring the house. But suddenly it bothered me – for the very first time – that the gutters along the roof were full of holes. And that the light shade above the front door looked like an ashtray from a cheap hotel. And that the garden wall was in urgent need of a coat of paint.

While the shutters hung neglected and dirty white outside the windows, all these flaws were part of the old stone house's character. But now the neat lavender-blue shutters had turned every charming flaw into an unendurable defect. Suddenly I knew, with a sinking feeling in my stomach, that we still had a lot of hard labour ahead of us.

Now another six months have passed. The garden wall has been painted (by myself) and the ugly light shade removed (by Alain) and the gutters will soon be replaced (by a professional person with a ladder that's even longer than the neighbour's). But in the meantime we've noticed a crack in the chimney, and the floor tiles in the big family bathroom are coming loose under our feet, which makes getting out of the bath quite dangerous, and the mistral has blown the garden gate right off its hinges, which means that all the dogs in the neighbourhood do their business under my rose tree at night. Every morning it becomes clearer that we need a new gate. Or a new rose tree.

Now I lie awake at night and wonder, while the mistral howls around the house and the dogs congregate in the garden, if the gate can wait until my dad's next visit. Then he can also advise us about the cracked chimney and the shifting bathroom floor. But that means I have to save up enough money to offer my dad another plane ticket. And that means I must stop studying hardware catalogues and write another book. And that, if I'm completely honest, is where the idea for this book came from.

Think of it this way. If you yourself bought the book you're now reading, then you've made a contribution to my new garden gate, for which I thank you in advance. Where else will my help come from?

15 Falling for autumn

'When is the best time to get to know Provence?' I am regularly asked by friends and strangers. 'Which season offers tourists the most?'

'The most what?' I always want to say in reply. 'The best time to get to know what in Provence?'

Every season in this region has its own joys and sorrows. Its unique combination of fantastic pros and unavoidable cons. Therefore it always feels like a trick question.

Fine, if it's the postcard picture of Provence that you want to see, then you must be here in July and August. When lavender and sunflowers turn the bare fields into a purple-and-yellow quilt. When bunches of grapes hang like heavy black hearts in the green vineyards and rambling roses stain the ancient stone walls pink and red. When the cicadas provide drowsy background music while you nap behind closed shutters at noon.

But if you don't like crowds of people, then at this time of year all the other tourists may get you down. If you're the kind of traveller who doesn't like to plan your journey ahead in the finest details, if you prefer to let impulse guide you, you'll probably struggle to find a place to stay. Never mind a place to park. And it can get really unpleasantly hot in the so-called lavender months.

If you don't like the heat, then it's better to come during the milder months on either side of The Season. May, June and September. Although we do sometimes experience an extraordinary heat wave towards the end of May. And although quite a few houses in our village were nearly washed away two years ago by an extraordinary rainstorm in September. See what I mean?

There is no such thing as an ideal time to visit Provence. It all depends. On the unpredictable weather, on your own more predictable habits, on your personality and your expectations and your whims and your fancies. If, like my friend Koos and my sister Hanna, you're above all interested in culinary climaxes, then it's quite a good idea to come early in May. Like them, you won't mind too much if it rains solidly for a week. You're going to spend all your time in food shops and restaurants, cheese boutiques and butchers, wine cellars and bars – and in your hostess's kitchen, of course, turning your willing hostess into a guinea pig for culinary experiments with local produce.

While Koos and Hanna were here, they didn't visit a single official 'tourist attraction' – until Hanna's efficient German husband arrived a week later and got everyone up early every morning to go and play tourist games. Visiting Roman ruins and medieval castles, strolling through the cobblestone lanes of picturesque villages, that sort of thing. Although I should add that after a few days even my Germanic brother-in-law was infected by the famous Mediterranean *laissez-faire*. A willingness to just hang around. Without necessarily *doing* anything.

For the more adventurous traveller I like to sing the praises of March and April. Yes, the weather is rather fickle, sometimes the winter sinks its teeth one last time into a landscape already dressed up for spring, but there is an unmistakable excitement in the air. The miracle of any new beginning, of rebirth, of resurrection. The region awakes from its long winter sleep, tiny new green leaves rustle on the bare plants and poplars, old men in berets polish their *boules* and start gathering on every square in every village, and the first tourists of The Season are welcomed with open arms. By the end of the season those arms become a little stiff, the legs a little weary from months of running around to please the tourists, and the smiles, well, not grim exactly, but not quite as hearty as a few months before either.

Early in the spring, every wine farmer and shopkeeper, every waiter and café owner, is still full of hope for the season ahead. Especially the hope that his bank balance will look better by the end of the season. But never mind the reason. For the tourist, what counts is that you can expect exceptionally good treatment in March and April.

For the true adventurer, the tourist who desires a unique experience, the traveller who has already experienced the picture postcard version of Provence, for them I would recommend the winter months without hesitation.

The south of France is not 'pretty' in winter. Not at any rate in the usual sense of the word 'pretty'. Unlike in the north of Europe, we have no soft green landscapes to enchant the winter tourist, no velvety hills and lush pine forests, not even a pristine white fairyland of snow. Yes, we are spoilt with a thin layer of snow every winter – even a thick layer in the mountainous areas – but the winter scenery is generally bare and dull. Bare branches scratching against bare stone walls, bare orchards, bare vineyards.

And yet. Just as the Karoo and the Kalahari have a unique power of attraction that you can experience but not explain, the bare landscape of this region has the power to enchant in unexpected ways. The vegetation may be predominantly grey and dull green, but the sky remains bright blue. Regularly. All the clouds blown away by the mistral and other winds. The light is more vivid than you'll ever find in the northern European winter. And this radiant light turns the olive plantations into silver visions.

Things you cannot see in summer take your breath away in winter. Like the pale trunks of the plane trees that are literally and figuratively put to shade by their lush green crowns in summer. The same way the antique stonewalls are often hidden by climbing plants in summer. Elbowed out of the spotlight by the gigantic shrubs of purple lavender and precocious yellow roses. In winter you can admire every bare stone in every bare wall.

More than anything else, Provence seems to me a place of stone. The simple stone walls of the houses; the impressive stone towers of the churches; the dilapidated packed-stone walls, without cement or any other binding material, that wind along the edges of fields and orchards; the uncomfortable stone seats in Roman amphitheatres; the stony ruins of castles and village gates. To really appreciate the stone, you have to be here in winter.

But of all the months, October is closest to my own heart. The loveliest, loveliest month – for reasons entirely different from those that made the poet Louis Leipoldt lyrical about the South African spring. In October, when autumn is in full swing, just before the winter starts to bite, peace descends on Earth and you can sense the goodwill around you. (Perhaps because the exhausting tourist season is finally drawing to a close.) There's a fresh sparkle in the air, the light has a coppery sheen and the vineyards and trees wear the most wonderful yellow and orange glow.

Or perhaps it's just that it was October when I first came here. We all know the enduring charm of first impressions. Ironically, I came here in October precisely because I wanted to avoid being swept off my feet. Precisely to avoid the summery postcard picture. Because I wanted to crawl inside the skin of the place rather than be seduced by the romantic surface.

And also, if I'm being completely honest, because I couldn't afford to rent even the tiniest cottage during the expensive summer months.

Perhaps it's time to explain how I was blown here by the winds of coincidence. I didn't arrive with the intention to settle here. I didn't even arrive because I wanted to be here, specifically. I wanted to spend a sabbatical year somewhere in the French or Italian countryside, it didn't really matter where, before my son started school in South Africa the following year. As everyone knows, when you have a child at school travel is restricted to school holidays. And I longed to spend an extended period in an unfamiliar environment, just one last time.

Little did I know.

I'd asked a few friends if they knew someone who might know someone who might have a cottage to rent. As fate would have it – and in this instance I really do believe that fate was throwing the dice – my friend Maré phoned a day later to say that she'd found a possible cottage. Somewhere in the French countryside. She didn't know where exactly. But it was no vague promise. Maré doesn't believe in vague promises. Maré believes in action. She'd already arranged for me to meet the owner of the cottage. The very next evening.

Suddenly – terrifyingly suddenly – the idea of a European sabbatical became a reality. I'd thought I would take months to look for a suitable and above all affordable place to stay. More than enough time to back out if I got cold feet. But I hadn't taken account of a friend like Maré's ability to take charge of other people's lives. (Thank you, Maré.)

After meeting Peta for a drink the next evening, the matter was settled. Peta showed us a few pictures of the cottage and the surroundings, and explained that she rented it out on a weekly basis in the summer months but was perfectly willing to let it to me for the autumn, winter and spring at a reduced long-term rate. When she added that she and her two young children had lived for a while in the house next door, where there was still a collection of toys and picture books available to keep my son busy, I didn't hesitate another moment.

The next day I remembered that I still didn't know *where* the cottage was.

Somewhere in the south of France, somewhere in the countryside, was all I knew. But it didn't matter. There'd be toys.

That's how I ended up in Provence. Because of toys, you might say. I did eventually find out where I was going, but there was no time to read up on the area. The organisational logistics of a year in a foreign country – if you're a single mother with a young child – made me run around like a headless chicken by day, and wake in a cold sweat at night. I had to find reliable tenants for my house in Stellenbosch, sell my car, cancel insurance policies, take out others and above all fill in dozens of official forms and gather stacks of paper in order to convince the French consulate to issue me a long-term visa.

It was my baptism of fire with the French bureaucracy. Had I known then that I'd still be chasing papers to satisfy French bureaucrats almost a decade later, I might have stayed where I was. Good thing one doesn't know.

But nothing was as bad as the packing. Everything my four-year-old son and I would need for a year had to be packed into two suitcases. Everything that couldn't fit had to stay behind. I spent weeks fretting over every item of clothing, every hairbrush (shouldn't I rather just take a comb? it takes up less space than a brush?), every dictionary I couldn't live without and every teddy bear my son couldn't live without.

They say the older and wiser you become, the more important it is to learn to take leave of possessions. To learn to travel increasingly light. If that is true, then in the weeks leading up to that French sabbatical I grew as old as Methuselah and as wise as Solomon.

But although there wasn't time for thorough research about my destination, I knew that I was on my way to a mythical place. The trouble with Provence is that its light and its landscape and its general atmosphere have captivated so many painters and writers and other famous people for so many centuries. You feel almost unworthy when you arrive, aware that you cannot follow in all those great footsteps. And rather unoriginal, too. Everything you can say, write and think about the place, has been said, written and thought by other, greater minds ages ago.

You have to remember that people have lived in the south of

France for centuries, building and cultivating for more than two thousand years. If you stand underneath the Pont du Gard near Nîmes – a majestic, slender aqueduct that was built to carry fresh mountain water to the Roman settlement – you cannot but admire this early civilisation's engineering prowess. A decade or so ago a catastrophic flood hit Vaison-la-Romaine, washing away numerous houses on the banks of the Ouvèze River and destroying bridges and roads, but the oldest bridge of all – the one built by the Romans – remained unharmed. They knew what they were doing, these Romans. Their bridges, like their amphitheatres, were built to last. You need to hear an opera in the amphitheatre at Orange just once to realise that they'd also mastered the secrets of acoustics. You can hear the proverbial pin drop on the stage, no matter how great the distance between your modest stone seat and the stage.

Around here you encounter the impressive remains of the Roman civilisation on a daily basis. The writer Lawrence Durrell, who lived here for more than 30 years until he died in his house in Sommières in 1990, collected his thoughts about Provence in a book with the telling title, *Caesar's Vast Ghost*. But you won't just run into the ghost of the Roman Caesar here. Numerous other great spirits have come, seen – and allowed themselves to be conquered.

One of the greatest of all, Albert Camus, lies buried in Lourmarin. Samuel Beckett lived just around the corner in Roussillon, a hillside village with unforgettable pink walls alongside an old ochre mine. Although the original Greek word *ôkhra* denotes yellow soil, the ochre mines of the Vaucluse have always yielded a rosy powder. And legend has it that Roussillon's soil owes its unusual red colour to the blood of Sirmonde the Beautiful ...

Sirmonde's powerful husband, Raymond, murdered her young troubadour lover and offered her the dead man's heart as a delicious meaty snack. When the beautiful Sirmonde realised what she'd eaten with such relish, she jumped from the nearest high cliff. The soil around the cliff has been unusually red ever since.

I didn't know this legend when I first came here. But I did know that numerous legends about the glorious days of the troubadours had their origins in this region. And the troubadours are probably just more proof that this region has always been irresistible to poetic souls. In the twelfth and thirteenth centuries the romantic word craft of troubadours like Raimbaut d'Orange, Raimbaut de Vacqueyras and Rainol d'Apt reigned supreme. Their names are recalled forever by the place names of Provence. Like the juicy melons of Cavaillon, the troubadour Gui de Cavaillon is part of that town's glory.

These days I know a lot more about the history of Provence. For example that Petrarch, who was attached to the papal palace in Avignon in the fourteenth century, became quite lyrical about the region and particularly about one of its inhabitants, the lovely Laure de Sade. Four centuries on, another De Sade became quite lyrical about other things. Even the libertine eighteenth century wouldn't tolerate the views expressed by this notorious aristocrat, who spent almost half his life in prison as a result. But when Donatien Alphonse François, the Marquis de Sade, didn't happen to be behind bars, he lived in his noble family's *château* here in the south – and appears to have made it a sought-after stopover for prostitutes, villains and decadent aristocrats en route between Marseille and Avignon.

Which just goes to show that life in the Provençal countryside hasn't always been all that quiet.

Even the famous Casanova made his way through the Provençal *campagne*, in the footsteps of his admired countryman Petrarch.

From the nineteenth century onwards, Charles Dickens and Henry James were among growing numbers of Anglo-Saxon writers who travelled through the region and expressed their admiration in letters and books. But in the twentieth century it was the painters who above all introduced a wider audience to the picture of Provence as we know it today. Among them there were those who were born here, like Paul Cézanne of Aix-en-Provence who developed a lifelong obsession with rendering a single beloved mountain peak with brush and paint. (He left behind more than sixty paintings of Mont Saint-Victoire.) And those who came from elsewhere, like the Dutchman Vincent van Gogh who painted the sunflowers and cornfields around Arles with almost equal obsession. Just ask any Japanese or American tourist to recall an image of Provence. Chances are that it'll be a picture of glowing yellow sunflowers. That intense, near-vibrating shade of yellow that Van Gogh regarded as symbolic of the south. The golden heart of Provence.

And then there were Gauguin, Picasso, Chagall ... you name them. Whether they came here on holiday or lived here for years on end, they were all captivated by the brilliant light. As certainly as a fly is captured in a spider's web.

When I came here, before I knew all the facts and anecdotes and legends, I already knew that Provence had a power of attraction beyond rational explanation. And I was determined to remain rational. I didn't want to become just another fly in the spider's web.

For that reason I was grateful that fate had arranged my arrival for the autumn. Grateful that I couldn't afford the irresistible summer months. Not for me the numbness of love-at-first-sight, thank you. I would gradually grow used to the environment, I decided, through the rainy days of autumn and the dull, bare weeks of winter and the windy months of spring. And when summer arrived at last, I would be armed with knowledge and experience. And if I was swept away nonetheless, in spite of all my careful precautions, well, then at least I'd be able to say that I didn't capitulate without a fight.

A bit like getting to know a man very well before you jump into bed with him. That was how I'd planned my relationship with Provence.

Ha!

The autumn enchanted me within days. That brilliant light on the glowing leaves. I wandered feverishly through villages and vineyards taking pictures constantly so that I would remember the colours of the leaves for the rest of my life. In winter the stones held me captive. The nakedness of the stone walls – but also a very specific stone that a naughty boy hurled through the window of my rented cottage. It led to an angry confrontation with the child's father. The boy was Hugo, the father was Alain, and the rest of the story, well, it continues to this day.

Alain was also a new arrival, a city dweller who was tired of life in the city, the only soul in this hamlet that I could really talk to. About books and music and movies and travels and 'the things of the soul that come first', as Simone de Beauvoir put it. His English was as poor as my French, but he could at least understand when I spoke English – just as I could understand his language better than I could speak it. We soon arrived at a practical compromise. We each simply carried on speaking in our own language. I spoke in my (second) language and he answered in his (first) language. And we learnt fast.

After all, the heart has its own language too.

That spring the wind blew harder than I've ever felt it since. Throughout the whole of April. And in May it rained all the time. And I couldn't have cared less. By then I was so in love – with the surroundings and with the man I'd come to know in these surroundings – that nothing could get me down. Except the idea that soon I would have to leave.

A few days before my departure at the beginning of July, Alain took me on a heartrending tour of the lavender and sunflower fields of the region. And I realised it was all true. Provence was a magical, mythical place.

I was indeed swept away, but not by the summer.

By the time summer came I was already as caught up as a fly in a spider's web.

This is why autumn still has a special magic for me. When autumn comes, when the vineyards around the village seem to burst in flame, when the plane tree starts to shed its leaves in our courtyard – as it's doing right now, while I sit here and write – then I always feel something of the excitement of that very first autumn stirring inside me. That numb, irrational, inexplicable phenomenon called love at first sight.

16 It's only words

It's rather difficult, in any language, in any country, to make a living from words. Mining Afrikaans words in the heart of Europe is an industry that probably borders on insanity. But a world without insanity would probably also be a duller place.

This is the challenge I face day after day. To continue living in France and to continue writing in Afrikaans.

I don't do it because I want to be a campaigner for the language, exactly. I do it because I cannot really do anything else.

Words have always been my bread and butter. Sometimes my jam, too. I've been a reporter on a daily newspaper, a features writer for a magazine, a copywriter, a proofreader, a sub-editor and a translator. Also a writer of children's books and youth books and a novelist. Words sustain me – literally and figuratively.

But here in Europe I soon discovered that words alone wouldn't fill my stomach. Not to mention my children's and my guests' stomachs. So what does an Afrikaans writer do in the French countryside when the hunger pangs begin to bother her? Well, she does something other than write. There has to be *something* else she can do.

Or that's what I thought.

There have been times in my life when I've worked, briefly, with something other than words. As a student I sometimes worked as a waitress to earn pocket money. I was a barmaid at a sports club for a while. Sold perfume in a department store in Pretoria one holiday. Later, during a yearlong ramble through Europe, I worked as a waitress again. In a Greek restaurant, this time. I washed dishes in the filthy kitchen of an insurance company in London. And I pushed a tea trolley through the endless corridors of another London firm: 'Cuppa tea, Sir? Milk, Ma'am?' And I was an *au pair* girl in France, a child minder.

That's the sum of my work experience, everything that's left if I take away the word business. Washing dishes, minding children, pouring drinks and waiting at tables. And selling perfume in Pretoria. All things I do anyway these days, without payment, like any mother living in Europe without domestic help. Except for flogging perfume, fortunately.

When I at last resorted to asking my friends via the Internet what an Afrikaans writer could do to earn pocket money in the French countryside, the only interesting suggestion anyone could come up with was phone sex.

I considered it briefly. Until I remembered that my French wasn't good enough. Oh well, Alain tried to console me, you don't need much of a vocabulary for a job like that. About twenty phrases and a variety of groans. Or maybe you could specialise in phone sex with foreign accents?

I suppose I could have gone to stand behind the counter in our local bar, but it really didn't appeal to me. When you're young, the garlicky moustaches of inebriated Frenchmen like Jean-Pierre might seem romantic. But at my age, garlic is garlic. And romance is, well, let's just say it's a lot scarcer than garlic.

No. When you consider the alternatives, playing host to strangers isn't all that bad. For this is one of the unexpected results of my life in the French countryside. I have entered the so-called hospitality industry.

The whole thing started with the inn I hired the second time I came to live in the French countryside. That was after I rented

Peta's cottage the first time, fell madly in love with the place and one of its residents, and after a year's torment in South Africa decided to return to Provence, boots and all. Maybe not forever, maybe just for a few years, we would wait and see what happened ...

I don't believe in signs and portents, but perhaps the inn was a sort of sign after all. It was the only affordable place I could find at short notice, a deserted hotel with the alluring name *L'Auberge Fleurie* (The Flower Inn) above the front door. And a long corridor with lots of rooms, each with a bed, wardrobe, table and chair, basin and shower, just as if the rooms were still waiting for the spirits of long-dead guests to return.

It was a hopelessly impractical home for a single mother with a single child. But after all the boring one-bedroomed flats the estate agent had tried to palm off onto us, this unusual home delighted my son and me right away. 'We can sleep in a different room every night!' Daniel exclaimed excitedly. And the corridor was long enough that he could roller-skate in it. So I signed the contract and we moved into the bohemian Flower Inn.

And somewhere in the back of my mind a flower seed was planted. If I cannot make my living from words, perhaps I could make it from beds? Perhaps rent out one of the rooms?

But first I'd have to do something about the décor.

Because every room had different coloured wallpaper – all unfortunately with the most awful patterns imaginable. We were soon talking about The Blue Room (mine), The Red Room (my office) or The Yellow Room (where Daniel slept most of the time, when he wasn't spending the night in the Green or the Pink Room, just for fun). As if we were living in an old-fashioned mansion or castle.

Of all these examples of wallpaper that you wouldn't dream of having in your house, the one in the long corridor was undoubtedly the worst. Massive orange, yellow and brown flowers with a vaguely psychedelic aura. Probably something acquired at a sale some time in the sixties. I couldn't help thinking of Oscar

Wilde's legendary last words. When he muttered that either the wallpaper or he would have to go. But I couldn't afford to replace the wallpaper – nor to die – so I simply tried to limit the damage by hiding as much of the orange flowers as possible behind Daniel's preschool art works, framed photographs, pictures and posters. Then it felt even more as if we were living in an old-fashioned mansion. With the long corridor as a sort of art gallery of dubious taste.

I know I sometimes exaggerate, just a little, for the sake of a juicier story. Therefore I don't blame the friends who thought it was just me exaggerating again when I complained about the wallpaper in an e-mail. But then a few of them came to stay at the inn. 'I see what you mean about the wallpaper,' Michiel murmured. Irna and the others clearly arrived at the same conclusion.

In the end it wasn't necessary to replace the wallpaper. A few months later Alain and I decided to put our eggs in one basket, however foolish that might seem at our advanced age, and I gave up the inn. And a year or three later, when we first walked into the stone house opposite the abbey, we knew right away that we'd found what we were looking for. That's how it is with houses, isn't it? Nothing to do with reliable wiring and other practical considerations. It's the atmosphere that strikes you, something in the air that wraps itself around your shoulders like a favourite old coat, and then you just know that your search has ended. You've come home.

Among the many attractions of this house, more for me than the rest of the family, was a big old barn from which the owner was then running an estate agency. Ah, I thought, this could be my studio! The proverbial 'room of my own' where I could write undisturbed!

But I knew that writing wasn't going to generate enough income to pay off the bond on the house. Then I discovered that the Flower Inn's seed had meanwhile taken root. Beds. Rooms. Accommodation. So we decided to transform the barn-cum-estate agency into a guest apartment that we could let on a weekly basis. To pay back our worried bank manager in the short term, but in the long term, hopefully, to earn an extra income one day.

And that is more or less the story of how I ended up in the hospitality industry. Put another way, if you live in this sunny tourist region, you play host to friends and family all summer long anyway. It's probably inevitable that at some point you'll see your way clear to do it for strangers too.

And it did end up being a more practical solution than phone sex.

So far the only unpleasant part of the business has been fixing up a little apartment inside the barn. Being once again at the mercy of French artisans. Not to mention their extended lunches. Or the bottles of *pastis* they consume at the end of every workday while delivering a detailed progress report at your kitchen table.

Sometimes there was no progress to report. Sometimes there was what you'd call decline, frankly. Like the time an impatient plumber chopped up all the terracotta tiles on the bathroom floor to lay the water pipes underground when the overseer had assured me that they'd be installed neatly along the wall. So we had to further increase our budget to buy new floor tiles. On days like those even the overseer, who usually drank only strong black coffee, knocked back a glass of *pastis*.

Or the time when the same impetuous plumber planted the toilet in the wrong place. Inside a cupboard. Well, it was going to become a cupboard, but at that stage there were still no shelves or a door and the next time I looked, there was the toilet solidly anchored inside the cupboard. With all the pipes already laid. Underneath the floor which had been chopped up even further for this purpose.

That day even I knocked back a glass of *pastis*.

What's done is done, Alain tried to console me. To now move the toilet – and all the pipes – would be a complete waste of time. We'd have to wait until the plumber was available again – which could be weeks from then – and in the meantime we couldn't replace the floor tiles or do anything else inside the bathroom. No, we'd just have to get used to a toilet inside a cupboard.

'They call it a WC, don't they?' Again my husband trying to cheer me up. 'A water closet? Well, here we've got a proper WC. With the emphasis on *closet*.'

I poured another glass of *pastis* and cursed all French artisans. A gross generalisation, I know, but by now I was fed up with the species. A few days earlier a charming carpenter had come to quote on the woodwork. I immediately christened him Monsieur Dali. Even in a country that's notorious for imposing moustaches (just think of Asterix, of José Bové, or, why not, of our own *pique-cul*, Jean-Pierre), his was a species that screamed for attention. Surrealistically long, absurdly thin, it curled smartly upwards on either side of his nose. Then I felt his hand on my bum – and remembered that there were other things for which Frenchmen were notorious. Our own *pique-cul* Jean-Pierre included.

I decided to look for another carpenter. Easier said than done. I was in a hurry. The carpenters in this area were not. Consider it just another cultural difference.

In the end I was forced to buy a readymade kitchen cupboard. And as the bathroom cupboard had meanwhile been eliminated by the plumber's blunder, I realised that the carpenter could in fact also be eliminated. We put up the remaining shelves in the apartment ourselves.

And so, from one crisis to the next, you might say from one *pastis* to another, the former barn was at last turned into a small apartment. A bedroom with a double bed, a combined sitting and dining room with a tiny kitchen in one corner, a bathroom with, well, let's just call it an interesting toilet. The work took a month longer than we'd hoped, but then we'd lived here long enough to know that it could've been much worse. After all, a month around here is just like a day in most other places.

In the meantime, the summer had arrived in all its glory and we were anxiously awaiting our first paying guests. The other guests would come anyway. We'd long stopped being anxious about them.

Of course there is a difference between guests who pay and guests who don't. For paying guests you iron the bed linen. The rest can sleep between unironed sheets. Paying guests are served dinner if they want to eat with you and they don't have to help set the table or wash the dishes. The rest you ask to pretend they're in their own homes. If they're thirsty they can make their own coffee or pour their own drink. If they're hungry they're welcome to look in the kitchen cupboards for a packet of almonds or a jar of olives. For paying guests you get up early, put on decent clothes and sweep the courtyard. When the rest are around, you shuffle around in your Egyptian kaftan without washing your face or combing your hair, until you've had your second cup of coffee.

In short, for strangers you make more effort.

Fortunately I don't have to do it every day. I don't like talking to strangers all the time. (I don't even like talking to friends all the time.) I still need quiet and solitude to write. That's why I prefer to live in a hamlet in the *campagne* rather than in a cosmopolitan city like Paris. Here the tourist season lasts only a couple of months, then along with winter a blessed silence descends over the landscape. In winter we stay indoors, we hibernate like bears, building up our energy for the exhausting summer months ahead.

And fortunately we're not on the route for instant tours of Europe. Our village is so tiny that most maps don't even mention it. It lies among world-famous vineyards and lavender fields and sunflowers, but far from trains and buses and public transport. You need your own wheels to get here. And you mustn't be in too much of a hurry.

Maybe it's the slow pace that makes foreigners seem less foreign. When they arrive, we don't know them at all. When they leave, they sometimes feel, well, a lot like the rest.

The other day a professor called from Britain just to say he'd arrived home safely. And a couple of French teachers mailed us a copy of an Italian novel we'd talked about late one night under the plane tree. And Santa from Stellenbosch sent a postcard from the next stop in her European tour. And a housewife from Hamburg sent word that she'd found the German translation of one of my books in a local store. The kind of thoughtfulness that you'd really only expect from family and friends.

I've discovered to my surprise that tourists are sometimes rather nice people. (I used to think of them mostly as an irritation because they occupied all the parking space in the village and bought up all the croissants in the bakery early in the morning.) I have to admit that I rather enjoy some of these encounters.

Or maybe it's just that I've finally realised you do need more than words to stay alive. Sometimes you also need people.

17   The kingdom of food

You cannot write about France without also writing about food. I cannot even think about France without also thinking about food. For me, France and food go together like a chicken and an egg. Both of which can probably also be considered food. The chicken and the egg, never mind which came first. See what I mean?

Like most of us I have always liked to eat well. But ever since I've been living in France, eating well has acquired a whole new meaning. It's not something that happens now and again, by chance and with a bit of luck, in a good restaurant. For the French, eating well, eating slowly, eating with pleasure, is a daily responsibility, the duty of every patriotic citizen, the unofficial national motto. Forget *liberté, égalité, fraternité.* It's a praiseworthy philosophy, but philosophy doesn't fill your stomach.

Recently, a Frenchwoman who's lived in South Africa for years confessed to me that if there's one thing that irritates her whenever she goes back to France, it's her French family's obsession with food. The entire day revolves around the buying of food, the preparation of food, the intake of food! No sooner has one meal ended than they start planning the next one!

I know what she means. What irritates me personally the most is the amount of washing up produced by these endless meals. At least three plates for every eater, and a whole collection of knives and forks for all the different dishes. But most of the time I am deeply grateful that I live in a country where food is a national obsession. Rather than guns, for example, or crime or cars.

As obsessions go, food is decidedly not the worst example that I can think of.

Since coming to live here, I've enjoyed the most magnificent meals of my life. And I don't just mean a few culinary climaxes in famous restaurants. Our family budget doesn't stretch to visits to famous restaurants. But about once a year, on a birthday or other significant date, my husband and I forget about our budget and spoil each other with a truly memorable meal in a truly stylish restaurant. Then we live on bread and cheese for the rest of the month – without a moment's regret. *Non, je ne regrette rien*, we murmur along with Piaf.

For weeks afterwards our mouths water whenever we remember our meal. We torture each other cruelly with our memories. A fish fillet's delicate flaky texture. The milky succulence of a slice of veal. The ecstasy of the *amuse-bouche* – a thimble of soup or a lick of pâté – which appears on the table unsolicited in-between the other dishes. And the vegetables – ah, those crunchy little vegetables!

No, we never regret our *gourmandise*.

And yet most of the magnificent meals I've enjoyed here have been somewhat simpler. And a lot more convivial. Not in restaurants. Not even in houses. I'm talking about open-air meals with friends. A long table with a white tablecloth, in someone's garden or on someone's verandah, under umbrellas or in the cool shade of plane trees or in silver moonlight. Some twenty guests, each of whom brings something to eat. Some bring the appetisers, others the starters, some the salads, others the cheese. Everyone makes an effort, it goes without saying, no one's going to stint when it comes to such a communal meal. But not so much effort that you arrive at the meal pale with exhaustion either. There's no need – there are so many delicatessens in the area that you can always buy something special if you don't want to make it yourself.

I usually end up in the dessert brigade. 'Ask Marita to bake a cake.' Funny, in South Africa, no one (least of all I) particularly admired my skill as a baker. But here, where even the tiniest village boasts an excellent bakery, women seem to have lost the ability to bake their own cakes. With the result that, mediocre baker though I am, I've been promoted to the A team overnight.

Madame Voisine, member of the endangered species of home bakers, thinks it's a scandal that her younger neighbours are no longer up to making something as simple and yet classical as a *tarte citron*. And on those rare occasions when they do bake a tart, they do it with readymade store-bought pastry! *Quelle horreur!* As she reprimanded me the other day when she caught me with a packet of readymade pastry in the queue at our local supermarket. I got a lecture on the secrets of a homemade *tarte citron* there and then.

Madame Voisine is what you might call a culinary dictator. The dough is mixed like this, not like that. You use this kind of almond, not that. And see, this is what the lemons must look like. This size, this exact shade of yellow. *Impeccable.*

I muttered weakly that I'd never attempted a lemon tart in my life. That I wasn't even the tart maker in our home. That I was here only to buy pastry for my husband who wanted to rustle up a quiche for lunch.

'*Votre mari?*' The thin pencil lines that serve as Madame Voisine's eyebrows shot up. A man who baked tarts? In that case, she said, with a sympathetic pat on my elbow, I might as well buy the readymade pastry.

It is true that I know nothing about tarts. But Alain's colleagues are crazy about my lopsided chocolate cakes. They think it's a traditional South African recipe, like milk tart or the jam tarts we call Hertzoggies: Marita's lopsided cakes. At first I blamed my ancient oven for the strange shapes of my home-baked cakes, but I stopped making excuses long ago. I just smile gracefully as I place another uneven cake among all the French delicacies on the table. And I watch amazed each time it's devoured by the fastidious French.

Of course, it's not just the food that makes these meals so special. It's also the laidback atmosphere, the leisureliness with which one dish is tasted after another, the generosity with which the wine is poured. The moonlight that makes everyone seem more beautiful. The sunlight, which is never so strong that your sweat starts to drip onto your plate. The music provided by a symphony of birds and insects. The sudden applause of leaves rustling in a breeze.

It was during one such moonlit meal that I first heard a nightingale sing. Truly an enchanting experience. But usually it's my friends at the table who start singing late at night. I can't sing along, because I don't know the words of the songs they've all grown up with. And yet I enjoy listening to their lingering and sometimes drunken voices. It's part of the whole hedonistic package – lovely scenery, delicious food, good wine, lively arguments, ridiculous behaviour – which turns an ordinary meal into an unforgettable occasion.

In our own house food is no less important than in most French homes. But in our multilingual, multinational family, food is also often a battleground of cultural differences. It's almost impossible to find anything that (a) everyone will eat and (b) everyone will eat in the same way.

Pancakes, for example, meet the first requirement – all children love pancakes. But Hugo insists on eating his the French way, with chocolate spread and folded into a triangle, while Daniel covers his with cinnamon sugar and rolls them up, the way we do in South Africa. And Mia, true to her mixed genes, wants both chocolate spread and cinnamon sugar on her pancakes. And if forced to choose, she subjects us to an ear-splitting identity crisis.

Or take something like cheese. They say you can contemplate the entire ocean in a drop of water, don't they? Well, then you can probably also observe our family's eating habits in a piece of cheese.

Daniel likes cheese that is sweet and bright yellow with a firm texture. His favourite is still the Gouda he got to know as a toddler in South Africa. His taste has hardly developed beyond that. On days when he's feeling really reckless, he might try a piece of Brie. While Thomas, on our family holiday in South Africa, searched desperately for anything other than the sweet, bright-yellow Gouda that you find in every supermarket. 'Where is the Comté, the Saint-Marcellin, the Fourme d'Ambert?' he kept asking. 'Where is the Roquefort, the Lou Perac, the Vieux Lille, the Bleu de Bresse?' In short, where was the cheese?

'This is the cheese, Thomas', I had to say over and over. 'This is the choice you have here.'

Gouda and Cheddar and a few other processed cheeses that according to him all tasted like plastic. I let him try a local Camembert. He burst out laughing.

No, Thomas is not a pretentious gourmet. He is a perfectly ordinary French teenager. He grew up with cheese, a wide variety of cheese, of colours and flavours and tastes and shapes. For him cheese is never just cheese. He'd never say, 'I really feel like a nice piece of cheese.' He'd be more specific. 'Can I have the last piece of Coulommiers?' No, if the truth were told, he will eat the last piece of Coulommiers without asking if anyone else might want it. As I said, he's a perfectly ordinary teenager, as selfish as any other.

However, the French blood flows so thick in my daughter's veins that no cheese has ever scared her. Sometimes, for example, Alain opens a Münster that's so atrociously ripe the aroma will make you faint with shock. Daniel will shrink from the table in horror. Hugo and Thomas will politely avert their refined French noses. Mia is the only one who will taste the cheese with Alain. Even if she does so holding her nose.

My own taste in cheese has come a long way since I first moved here. I still struggle with the flavours at times, but I've learnt to hide my aversion. I've learnt the knack of shutting my nostrils subtly without using my hands, a bit like an undertaker working on a decomposing body. It took a lot of practice, but I didn't really have a choice. I was thrown in at the deep end soon after my arrival.

A few of Alain's friends had come to visit from Lille – with a very special gift for the new woman in his life. Their home town's most famous contribution to the French cheese industry is called Vieux Lille. Old Lille – with the emphasis, definitely, on old. Old as in smelly, as in sweaty sports shoes, as in mouldy laundry baskets. (Please note that this is my description. No lover of Vieux Lille would ever concur.) Alain's friends proudly handed me the cheese, closed inside three Tupperware containers to prevent the aroma from escaping. When I opened the third and final container, and the flavour burst forth like an evil spirit, I realised that I was dealing with a Trojan horse. This was no innocent gift, it was more like a kind of test. Like a ritual initiation into a secret organisation: 'If you can eat this, we'll accept you as one of our own.' That was the underlying message.

I ate the cheese. I even pretended to like it. It was a dramatic tour de force. (At that stage, remember, I had such limited experience of cheese that even a mature Cheddar was something of a challenge.) These days I can honestly say that I've learnt to eat Vieux Lille. Not to like it, just to eat it without automatically grabbing my nose. On condition that the flavour hasn't had the chance to really 'develop'. In other words, when it stinks like ordinary smelly socks, instead of smelly socks that a piece of rotten meat has been wrapped in.

This must be what is meant by an acquired taste. Lynn the Farmer, for instance, is mad about Vieux Lille. But then she has lived in France for much longer than I have. So there is still hope for me.

Of all the cultural gaps that exist between members of our family – language, religion, history, general background – the food gap frustrates me most on a daily basis.

For example: Daniel has eaten most vegetables since he was small, except for eggplant and baby marrow, which he hates with a vengeance. Thomas and Hugo do eat *aubergines* and *courgettes*, as they call them, but despise most other vegetables. Except for tomatoes. Everyone in the house loves tomatoes. Except Mia. Unfortunately, eggplant and baby marrows and tomatoes are the basic ingredients of some of the most delicious traditional dishes of the region. Like *ratatouille*, like *tian*, like *farcis provençaux*. So whenever Alain and I want to spoil our guests or ourselves with a special Provençal dish, at least half of our children are sulking.

Further example: Daniel and Mia like cauliflower and broccoli and even, believe it or not, cabbage. Thomas and Hugo hate cauliflower and broccoli and, above all, cabbage. All four refuse to eat Brussels sprouts. (I suppose that's not so strange. I've never met a child who liked Brussels sprouts.) Daniel doesn't like pork or ham or anything else that's even vaguely connected to pigs. That includes the famous dried sausages from various French regions, as well as the incredible variety of pâtés available everywhere. To not like pâté, in a country that has elevated pâté to an art form, is a disaster if you ask me. But my son didn't ask me. He made up his own mind about not liking pâté, and that's that. While the other three children can't get enough of the dried sausage and pâtés.

In summary. We live in a kingdom of food – and the only thing all our children and all their friends like equally is American fast food. Hamburgers and chips. Chicken nuggets and fish fingers. And frozen store-bought pizzas. It breaks my heart.

Alain and I eat just about everything, but even we have our culinary differences. Alain adores tripe and animal intestines, while I will eat it only if there's really nothing else available. And I always feel slightly nauseous watching him eat a gruesome piece of blood sausage. I have tasted it. I believe in trying everything and holding on to that which is good. It's just that blood sausage is not part of that which is good and that which I want to hold onto.

I would like to call myself an adventurous eater. Anyone who wants to move to another country needs a strong sense of adventure. If you don't like what you don't know, then best stay where you are. And a sense of adventure often starts with something as basic as food.

If you voluntarily expose yourself to strange tastes, unfamiliar textures, unusual combinations, then food can become a fantastic adventure. You'll be challenged, you'll be charmed and sometimes terrified, you'll be disappointed at times and surprised, often. As with any adventure.

Well, that's what I try to teach our children. So far with very little success.

There's really only one kind of food that's loved by our entire family, and that's the humble potato. We eat sacks of potatoes in this house. We eat it boiled in the skin, baked in the oven, chopped into Spanish omelettes, cut into strips as *frites*, smashed into mashed potatoes, spread over mince as shepherd's pie, sliced and sprinkled with cheese as *gratin*, as salad with olive oil ...

But wait, there is another thing, a little more surprising, that is loved by the lot of us. We are formidable eaters of artichokes. Arti-*what*? As my brother asked when he came to visit. Within a few meals, though, he'd succumbed to our artichokes. By the third week he went to fetch his own fresh artichokes from the market and cooked them in our kitchen. Back in South Africa he suffered severe withdrawal symptoms for a while.

Like my friend Terry, who was highly indignant to discover that she could buy only canned artichokes back in Stellenbosch. Well, it *was* winter in Stellenbosch. But even in summer you're not likely to find this vegetable at the nearest corner café.

Here you find it in abundance almost throughout the year, in just about every shop. Cheap, too (the main reason why our large family eats it so regularly), and ridiculously easy to prepare (the other important reason). We simply toss the artichokes into boiling water, remove them before they're cooked to a pulp, and serve them just like that. With a bit of mayonnaise to dunk each little leaf on its own. Absolutely irresistible.

There's another local product for which our region is world-famous, but unfortunately not one with which I seduce my friends because it's anything but abundant and certainly not cheap. It's a black bulb with an overpowering aroma and a unique taste that hides in the soil beneath certain oak trees. It's a kind of fungus, they say, a super-special mushroom. Yes, if you've ever tasted it, you'll know that I'm talking about truffles. The sought-after *Tuber melanosporum*, to be botanically precise.

The biggest truffle market in Europe is held around the corner in Richerenches every Saturday morning, from the end of November until the beginning of April. In nearby Saint-Paul-Trois-Châteaux a truffle festival is celebrated every February with a majestic and massive truffle omelette. In Grignan, with its romantic château, the winter is ushered in every year with a festival of wine and truffles.

This is where the owners and chefs of Europe's greatest restaurants and delicatessens come to buy their truffles. In cash, with stacks of banknotes as thick as bricks, because the truffle market is traditionally a black market. An unofficial business from which many farmers earn a tax-free income. You can't really blame them. Truffles aren't a visible harvest, such as vineyards or olive plantations. Not a single leaf or twig sticks up above the ground. You need a trained dog or pig to sniff them out. So why pay the government for something the government cannot see?

I gather that's the argument more or less.

But what is all the fuss about really? That's what friends and strangers keep asking me. I am considered a truffle expert simply because I live among the truffles. It's a little like considering someone an astronomer simply because they live under the stars, isn't it?

But never mind, I'll give you my humble opinion.

Truffles are like dope. Once you've had the smell in your nostrils, you will always recognise it from a distance. Regular truffle eaters, like regular dope smokers, believe they know some secret of the universe that the rest of mankind has yet to learn. So many myths have therefore evolved around the use of this substance that the first taste is often an enormous disappointment. At any rate that's my experience. Of truffles and of dope.

And yet I won't deny that there is something special about a fresh truffle. Even if it's just that it's so expensive that you feel as if you're eating your wedding ring. It's not called 'black gold' for nothing.

Forget about the bottled version, Madame Voisine sniffs. Don't even taste it, says the little food dictator. You might just as well taste one of those sickly sweet glacé cherries from the little box and try to convince yourself that's what a fresh cherry from a tree tastes like.

It's easy for her to talk. She doesn't have to pay for fresh truffles. One of her relatives owns a piece of land where the right kind of oak tree grows – and relatives help each other out, don't they?

I was also lucky, in my first year in Provence, to taste fresh truffles several times without having to pawn one of my modest pieces of jewellery for the privilege. My neighbour hunted for truffles himself, with the help of a friend's trained dog, and was sometimes kind enough to share his find with me. After the first time he'd offered me the little black bulb, I was one of the initi- ated who would recognise the nose-deadening flavour for the rest of my life. And because my house and his had previously been one, with a paper-thin wall in the passage to create two separate units, I always knew right away when he'd gone to find truffles.

The aroma simply drifted through the wall in the passage. Sometimes it hung over the entire house like a suffocating cloud. All it took, when I saw my neighbour in the street, was to inno- cently remark that the scent of truffles was in the air. Then he looked guilty right away and offered me a piece.

I suppose it's possible that he may have had other motives. Like any warm-blooded, single Frenchman he was fairly interest- ed in the temporary female company on the other side of the pas- sage wall. For all I know, he was trying to seduce me with truffles.

They are after all about as expensive as diamonds.

But by then I was already being seduced by another Frenchman. With neither truffles nor diamonds.

These days Alain and I sometimes eat a sliver of fresh truffle in an omelette or a bowl of pasta, but it remains a rare luxury. We haven't managed to turn our loving black-brown mongrel into a truffle hound. Lily likes sniffing around rubbish bins more than sniffing under oak trees.

And I honestly cannot say that I miss truffles in my diet. There are enough other dishes in this food kingdom to ensure that eating will remain a daily adventure for years to come.

18   Postal pleasures

My roots are in South Africa, as a fellow expatriate put it, but my branches and leaves are in another country. That's the best description I've so far heard of what it feels like to be spread across two countries. Please note that I say spread, not torn. A tree with its roots in one place and its branches in another is not a torn tree. It is an exceptionally wide-reaching tree.

Take the plane tree outside our house for example. Its roots have been firmly anchored for decades in the street beyond our garden wall, which suits me very well, thank you, because it means that the municipality takes care of it, prunes it thoroughly once every two years, protects it against disease and vandals. But its branches and leaves hang over our own tiny courtyard and provides the loveliest shade for our family and all our guests every summer.

For me this plane tree therefore offers only pleasure, without any unpleasant duties. I do have to sweep the courtyard regularly in autumn if I don't want to drown in the enormous brown leaves it shakes off so recklessly. But it's a small price to pay for the glorious green shade in the summer months.

For me this plane tree isn't just any old tree. It's 'my tree' – although of course it doesn't belong to me. It's also a metaphor for my life in my adopted country. My leaves and my branches thrive beneath the high blue sky above Provence, but my roots will always be nurtured elsewhere. Beyond the garden wall.

We South African expatriates all have our separate ways of keeping our roots from withering. We subscribe to South African magazines, we listen to South African music (far more than when we lived in South Africa), we bake our own buttermilk rusks or teach an overseas butcher to make boerewors, we stay in touch via the Internet and e-mail, we get together with other South African souls abroad. The latter in moderation, in my case. I don't of course have a wide variety to choose from in the French country-side. Unlike in London – where these days you can talk about Little Madibaland the way New Yorkers talk about Little Italy – here in Provence South African company is as scarce as red jelly.

And it suits me this way. I would've liked to see more red jelly, for the children's sake, but the shortage of South African company has never bothered me. I don't understand the congregating of South Africans in cities like London or Sydney. If your entire social circle, from pub to church, is confined to other South Africans, then surely you're shutting yourself off from the people and customs and quirks of your adopted country? Sounds to me like a rather shortsighted option. Sounds to me as if you're losing more than you've gained.

Put another way, you become so obsessed with your roots that you don't even notice that your branches and leaves are wilting.

The most reliable recipe for healthy roots remains an occa-sional journey to your native land. To feel the ancient dust of Africa between your bare toes. To smell the scrub bushland of Riversdale or the bamboo at Franskraal. To admire Table Mountain's blue silhouette over the rim of a glass of Meerlust Rubicon. Not on a postcard or a picture in a magazine or a pho-tograph on your computer screen. But to actually be there.

I don't think I would've adjusted so easily in the French coun-tryside if I hadn't returned regularly to where I come from. At least twice a year, if at all possible. I realise I'm privileged because many of my journeys are paid for by a publisher who wants me

to come and promote a book or by a university that invites me to
give a few lectures. Because even on the busiest promotional tour
there is time for an evening around a table with old friends.

But yes, even though I am lucky enough to mix business with
pleasure on most of my journeys, there is a large part of the year
left when I'm not travelling. An awful lot of dull days when I am
here – and almost everyone I care about is over there. It's days
like these that have taught me to value the post like never before.

If you live in another country, the post becomes as important as
an umbilical cord for an unborn baby. Or a rescue rope for a
drowning person. A lifeline between here and there, between danger and safety, between the foreign and the familiar.

Like most expatriates I depend on mail. Mostly on electronic
mail these days, because it's so effortlessly immediate. Like picking up the phone, but without the worry that you might reach the
person on the other end at an inconvenient moment. And without
the fatal cost of a phone call to another continent.

Much better than a telephone really. After all, you cannot
phone all your friends and relatives at once, but you can send any
important news in a communal letter via the Internet. Granted,
this sometimes irritates those friends who require a more personal kind of attention. But anyone who has lived for a time in
another country knows that you cannot repeat everything that
happens to you twenty times to twenty different people.
Communal letters are like parties in cyberspace, virtual gather-
ings where you can exchange news with a lot of people at once.
The best of all is that there are no dishes to clean afterwards.
Come to think of it, of all the modern conveniences in my
European house the most indispensable are probably (a) my dish-
washer and (b) my Internet connection.

But let's not forget about the miracle of ordinary old-
fashioned post. It seldom happens these days that one comes
across a real letter in a real post box. A letter on paper, in the
familiar handwriting of a loved one, carefully sealed inside an

envelope with lots of colourful stamps on it. And the scarcer such letters become, the more exciting it becomes to receive one. If the envelope bulges pleasantly because a few photographs or newspaper cuttings have also been stuffed inside, then a simple postbox turns into a Christmas stocking on any day of the year.

Not to mention the pleasure of a parcel. When the postman knocks on the front door with a parcel that's too big to fit through the slot in the postbox, everyone in the house immediately comes running. They're often just copies of my books sent by publishers. Which warms my own heart, of course, but leaves the rest of the family completely cold. They are always hoping for something more interesting.

Like the biltong my dad sometimes sends from the Cape. (The French half of my family likes biltong even more than the South African half.) Or the Grandpa powders and Tums tablets sent by Rose from Pretoria because Alain believes that nothing in France cures his headache or his indigestion faster. (Yes, even medicine gets us excited when it arrives via the post. Anything in a parcel instantly acquires an irresistible allure.) Or the exotic spices which Mario sends from Réunion. Or the latest Harry Potter which Irma sends from Cambridge, before it's been translated into French or Afrikaans, so that Daniel and Hugo can boast to their friends that they know who's dying this time ...

Our parcels come from all over the world, because these days our friends and family are spread all over the world. Madame Voisine always asks me to save the stamps for her. I suspect she doesn't really collect stamps. I suspect it's just another way to satisfy her insatiable curiosity about her neighbours. She wants to know where their post comes from.

Because of these international postal articles I've developed quite an intimate relationship with a number of postal employees by now. It might be pure coincidence, but if I had to make a list of the most interesting characters I've met in France, there'd be at least two postwomen on it. Just below Madame Voisine's name, probably.

Here in the countryside the postmen are usually women. Not *facteurs* but *factrices*. They wear dark-blue all-weather jackets and drive bright-yellow little station wagons (think of the colour of American school buses) or ride on noisy scooters. And many of them appear to be dyslexic.

At least that is the only logical explanation for their inability to distinguish between my strange foreign name and other strange foreign names. During our first year in Church Street, any postal article addressed to anyone with a vaguely Germanic name was delivered to us. We regularly received electricity bills and local tax forms and postcards intended for a retired Flemish couple at the opposite end of the village, or for the German owners of a luxury holiday home, or even for ordinary French citizens with non-French surnames such as Vollemaere or Vyncke.

I complained. I asked Daniel to paint *Van der Vyver* in fat black letters on our postbox. I carried the stray envelopes back to the post office to go and explain that Van der Vyver was different from Vandenbroeck. I kept watch at the kitchen window for an entire morning to intercept the *factrice* the moment her scooter stopped outside in the street. So that I could return a stack of envelopes to her, so that she could deliver them to the right addresses (clearly written on each envelope). For all my trouble it still took about a year for the stream of unwanted letters to dry up.

And then the *factrice* went on vacation.

And the woman who came to work in her place began to deliver envelopes with Polish and Slavic names to our address.

The temporary *factrice* didn't just have a reading problem, she also had a voice. The kind of voice you'd expect from an overweight, old-fashioned actress, not a sinewy and flat-chested post-woman. If she wasn't sure about a postal article's proper destination, she would sit on her scooter outside our garden gate and roar like a wartime canon: *Il y a quelqu'un?* Two separate, deafening salvos. *Il ya. Quelqu'un?* (Is anyone home?) One stiflingly hot summer day when I was indeed home but unwilling to interrupt my *sieste* to negotiate with the *factrice*, I pretended I wasn't there. She'd have to come back the next day anyway, I reasoned, we could sort the matter out then.

But I hadn't reckoned with this postwoman's reckless determination. After she'd roared loudly enough to wake the dead in the local graveyard, she burst into the holiday flat next door like a veritable Gestapo officer. Here the French couple to whom we'd let the flat for three weeks were lying stark naked on the bed, fast asleep. (Or rather, they'd been asleep until the *factrice*'s voice disturbed everyone in the entire street. Or that's what they told us later. Perhaps they weren't sleeping at all.) Be that as it may, our tenants grabbed sheets and items of clothing in alarm, but the *factrice* hardly seemed to notice that they were naked. She didn't apologise, she didn't offer to wait outside while they got dressed, she just wanted to know if this envelope wasn't perhaps intended for them. And she shoved the envelope under their noses. They shook their heads, speechless with shock, and the *factrice* turned on her heel and marched out of the door without any further explanation.

The French couple related this bizarre encounter over a glass of *pastis* that same night. By then they were no longer shocked, more amused, really, by our strange postwoman. (I had begun to suspect that all French postal employees were fairly odd, but our tenants assured us that ours was odder than the rest.) They saw the whole thing as a delightful holiday anecdote with which they would later amuse their friends.

For me it was a thornier matter.

I began to lock our front door when we took our afternoon nap. A strange irony. Living here, I have never been scared of burglars or any kind of intruders. In our previous house the front door key got lost at some point and for several months we lived happily without a key. For a paranoid South African like me, this absence of fear is one of the greatest joys of my current existence. But now I was suddenly afraid that our eccentric temporary postwoman might burst into our bedroom unexpectedly.

And yet she wasn't the strangest postwoman I've met here. That honour belongs to the one with a dog phobia in our previous village. I'm not talking about an ordinary wariness of barking animals. That is after all something one would expect from someone who encounters a wide variety of dogs in the daily performance of her duties. I also don't mean an extreme irritation with dogs and their indignant barking. No, this woman had a deep-seated and overwhelming fear of any dog. Even the most lovable fluffy puppy made her break out in a sweat. I'm talking about the sort of phobia that requires psychological treatment. Except that this woman did not go to a psychologist. She went to the post office and became a *factrice*.

A *factrice* with a fear of dogs is about as useful as a pilot with a fear of heights.

She refused to deliver our mail if Lily, our aged and gentle stray, wasn't locked inside the house. We tried to convince her that Lily had never been locked inside anywhere, that she wandered through the village streets like a tramp all day long, that old and young knew her and stroked and trusted her. The *factrice* refused to be convinced.

We tried to lock Lily inside, even if it was only during the morning, when the *factrice* was expected, but there was always a child or a child's friend who left one of the side doors open. (This was the house with the front door with no key, remember. Friends and strangers simply walked inside. And didn't always check that the door was closed when they walked out again.) Lily escaped every morning. Even when we couldn't find an open door anywhere, Lily managed to escape. At one point I wondered if she might be climbing out of the second-storey window and hiding the ladder somewhere in the street. The Houdini of dogs, that's what Lily had become.

And I became my own postwoman.

The *factrice* worked out a sadistic routine to punish me for having a wandering dog. She parked her bright-yellow station wagon outside the house and hooted twice, loudly. Then I had to run outside to fetch the mail while she sat calmly behind the steering wheel. And when I say run, I mean run. My workroom was on a different storey right at the back of the house and if I didn't pitch up outside within 10 seconds, she simply drove off. Sometimes I was in the bathroom, or busy feeding the baby, or in the middle of the finest sentence I'd ever composed on my computer screen. The *factrice* couldn't care less. She drove off – and often stayed away the next day too. Just to make perfectly sure that I knew who was calling the shots in this relationship. Sometimes we received a whole stack of overdue mail just once a week. Sometimes important postal articles disappeared without a trace.

We complained at the post office. We heard that we weren't the only ones. Even at houses where there were no dogs, the *factrice* had started refusing to get out of her car. Imagine all the energy she saved. Her own energy, I mean, because from the residents she expected exceptionally energetic co-operation. The faster we all managed to get to her car, the sooner she'd be done with her daily round.

After a few months I was so irritated with her impatient hooting that I began to suspect the whole dog phobia had never been anything more than a devious way of avoiding her duty.

But it's apparently no simple matter to dismiss a French *factrice*. Not even one with a fake fear of dogs. The next thing you know, there might be a countrywide postal strike – just because the residents of your little village are too lazy to fetch their own post out in the street.

So I had to learn to live with the *factrice*'s hooting.

It would probably be an exaggeration to say that it was to get away from the postwoman that we left this village. But it was an enormous relief when we found a house in a different village. A joy to meet a different postwoman who wasn't afraid of dogs. Even if she was dyslexic.

By now she has learnt to read my strange surname. After a year and a half in Church Street we only occasionally find a stray envelope in our postbox. The post has once again become a pleasure. Although I still lock the front door when we take an afternoon nap. Not because I'm afraid of burglars; simply because there might be a temporary *factrice* lurking out there.

19 Under the weather

Long ago, in my previous life in another country, I believed that people who constantly talked about the weather were to be pitied. Just imagine how dull your life must be if the weather is the most interesting topic you can come up with. There are so many other things to get excited about! Literature and music, puddings and planets and politics. Or the neighbour's affair with someone else's wife, for that matter.

That was before I came to live in France.

During the first year or so all my most interesting conversations were about the weather. Chiefly because I lacked the vocabulary to wax lyrical about literature or gossip about the neighbour. The weather is a godsend for anyone who is struggling with a foreign language. You learn a few phrases off by heart and use them over and over. *Il fait beau! Quelle pluie! Ça caille! Ça souffle!* (Nice day, isn't it? Heavens, look at the rain. It's freezing cold! My, but it's windy today!) The best of all is that the phrase doesn't even have to match the weather. If on a steaming hot day you said '*Ça caille*' – as I initially did because I didn't know any better – your conversation partner would probably admire your ironic wit and reply in the same tone.

The French love this sort of humour. They call it *second degré*. In the first degree, you apparently mean everything you say. In the second degree you mean the opposite of what you say. *Second degré* has allowed me to get away with the most dreadful linguistic gaffes without anyone being the wiser.

Now that I've lived here a few years – and my vocabulary extends a little further than sun, rain and wind – I continue to occupy myself regularly with meteorological discussions. If I don't know what to say to the baker or the *factrice* or to the other mothers waiting at the school gate, the weather is something I can rely on. Partly because I don't know which books the baker has read or what music the *factrice* listens to or which political parties the other mothers support. The weather is safe. There cannot be too many serious disagreements when the weather is under discussion.

But at the same time – and I've had to come to the French countryside to learn this – the weather can be dangerous.

The people in our village are intensely interested in the weather because many of them make their living from either agriculture or the tourist industry, and in both these sectors the weather evidently plays a cardinal role. But whatever business you're in, around here you always keep an eye on the clouds. The weather can severely disrupt your everyday life. Here, as in other parts of Europe, the weather regularly swings between catastrophic extremes. Nowadays more regularly than ever, Madame Voisine likes to announce with a grim expression.

It can become deadly hot in summer. And when I say deadly I mean literally deadly. Last summer, thousands of elderly French succumbed in an unprecedented heat wave. And because Madame Voisine's ever invisible husband is already rather elderly, these deaths upset her very much. Madame is also no spring chicken, but she refuses to consider herself an old hen. Besides, she was born in the south, she is used to the heat, while poor Monsieur has the delicate constitution of a *Parisien*. As well as the laziness of a *Parisien*, according to the village gossips.

After the hot summer come the autumn rains, regularly, which wash away bridges and roads and cars. And then come the winter storms, regularly, which fell ancient trees, sink oil tankers at sea and stain the beaches black, cut the power and water supply in hundreds of towns. And we haven't even mentioned the snow, which causes massive traffic jams, halts trains and grounds aeroplanes and keeps people trapped inside their homes.

In my previous life I never really bothered about the weather. The wet Cape winters sometimes made it difficult to get the washing dry, and if the southeaster blew for three days at a stretch, I complained along with everyone else. Just out of habit. The hottest I'd ever been was for a few days in February in Stellenbosch. And the coldest a few days in July, during the annual arts festival in Grahamstown.

But since living here I've had so many unpleasant experiences with the weather that I watch the *météo* every night on TV. Even if I miss the rest of the eight o'clock news, I make sure that I'm there for the final few minutes when the weather is forecast for the next few days. It's almost like family prayers in the old days. The children keep quiet and the grown-ups concentrate.

I've also learnt to study the sky, to note the colour of the clouds and the direction of the wind, to try to gauge sudden changes in temperature. To be prepared for whatever catastrophe may come next.

By now I could present a seminar on weather catastrophes. Wind and lightning and cloudbursts, hail and frost and snow, you name them, I know the awful consequences of all these natural phenomena. My last computer was destroyed by lightning. Because I refused to listen when Alain warned me to disconnect the computer and the telephone whenever a thunderstorm raged overhead. Because it reminded me too much of my frightened grandmother who covered all the mirrors in the house and hid all the silver cutlery every time she heard thunder. I'm different from my grandmother, I thought, I'm not afraid of lightning.

I was taught an expensive lesson. Now I pull the (new) computer's plug out of the socket as soon as I hear thunder in the distance. Overcautious, that's what I've become. The thunderstorms in this region are really impressive, even for someone not easily frightened by lightning. Just the other day the general dealer in the neighbouring village – a helpful and smiling young man – was hit by a lightning bolt while playing soccer for the local team. Dead on the spot. Of course I've always known that lightning can be deadly, but I've never actually been acquainted with anyone who was killed this way. Just as I've never lost a computer to lightning before.

Our village's power supply is regularly interrupted by thunderstorms, wild winds or cloudbursts. We make sure that there are always candles in the kitchen and a torch in the drawer next to the fridge. But even so we're occasionally caught offside.

Like the time at the end of last summer when we returned from our compulsory camping holiday – compulsory because we had let our house to friends of friends for two weeks and quickly had to find another place to stay – and were hit by a dreadful hailstorm along the road. Hailstones the size of the proverbial chicken eggs. We had to shelter under a bridge for a while to protect the luggage on the roof from the assault. When we opened the garden gate, we noticed that the hail had wiped out Alain's baby tomato plants, tearing off the branches, and scattering the tiny red fruit on the ground like marbles. When we unlocked the front door we noticed that the power had been wiped out too. It was nearly dark and the children were starving after the long journey and I urgently had to make supper, but the tenants had used up all the candles and stored every single plate, glass and saucepan in a new place. And the torch batteries were flat.

Welcome home, Alain grinned while I tried to cook a packet of instant soup over a gas flame in the dark. He has a wonderful ability to maintain his sense of irony even in the most chaotic circumstances. I don't.

Snow causes trouble of a different kind. Not so much because it turns your house into a prison as the roads become impassable, or because, if you come from Africa, you're too scared to drive on snow anyway. No, I'm referring to the injuries and expense that accompany the snow. For our family, at any rate, every decent snowfall inevitably means an accident. Maybe we are just unlucky.

As by now you may suspect.

Like the time my mother got something stuck in her throat and slowly started turning blue. It was my first winter here, in that first little rented cottage, with no central heating and without a telephone. When it started to snow the day after Christmas, Daniel and I were still such novices and so excited that we didn't even feel the cold inside the house. But when it hadn't stopped snowing by New Year's Day a week later, we were a good deal less excited and the cottage was bitterly cold. And then my mother choked on a bread crust.

I grabbed her from behind in a wrestling grip and pushed both fists against her chest the way I'd been taught in a first aid course during my school years, and managed to dislodge a few crumbs in her throat. But something had stayed behind, because she kept coughing and spluttering and was soon struggling to breathe.

There were only three people in the house. My mother, four-year-old Daniel and me. I couldn't leave my mother and Daniel in the house and run to the neighbour to call an ambulance because I was afraid she would die while I was on the phone, before Daniel's horrified eyes. I also couldn't drag Daniel through the snow with me and leave my mother to choke on her own. And I couldn't send Daniel to phone because he was too small.

Above all, I couldn't worry about my decision for too long. Not when I saw the strange colour of my mother's face. So I ordered Daniel to keep giving her water, just to keep him busy, really, and ploughed through the snow to my neighbour's house. After I'd called the emergency number, I held my mother's hand while we waited for the ambulance.

We waited a long time. It was New Year's Day, most medical staff were on holiday and all the roads were covered in snow. After a while my mother started to breathe more easily. When the ambulance finally skidded up to our door, the crisis was over. My mother wasn't blue any more. She was now as white as the snow outside. So was I, unhealthily pale with fright.

I've never been able to greet a thick layer of snow with child-like excitement since. I've become distrustful of snow. And my distrust has, sadly, been confirmed by several subsequent experiences.

The week before Mia was born, when the incessant snow made me fear that I'd be forced to give birth at home. The morning when Thomas slipped on the ice outside the house and split open his chin. The time my teacher husband went skiing with a group of his pupils and came home with three broken ribs. Not a glamorous skiing accident. He fell from the ski lift – those moving little seats that are hoisted up the mountain with a cable – even before he had a chance to fasten his skis properly. We are not a family that can boast of glamorous accidents.

One morning that same week, when Alain was still laid up with his broken ribs at the ski resort, I asked Daniel to scrape the ice from the car's back window before I drove him to school. He scraped too hard. Or something. I've still not been able to figure out exactly what happened. All I know is that moments later the window was completely shattered.

Yet another unglamorous accident. When I dropped him off at school an hour late, the broken window was covered with a flapping sheet of plastic that had been stuck down hastily with sticky tape. Every few kilometres the wind tore the plastic loose, and then I'd have to stop, grab the sticky tape on the seat next to me, and stick it down all over again. I expected Daniel to be panic-stricken because he hated being late for school, but on this morning he seemed for some or other reason strangely resigned to his fate.

The next morning I discovered the reason why. He asked me to drop him off a few streets away from the school because he didn't want the other children to see this spectacle of a car with an improvised plastic window.

The morning before, he hadn't minded being late because the other children would all be inside their classrooms already.

It did look a little Third World, I suppose, this ancient car with a flapping sheet of plastic where the window was meant to be. And he is sometimes a little too sensitive about his Third World origins. So I bit my tongue and dropped him off out of sight of the school grounds.

As for me, the longer I live here in the First World with its impossible weather patterns, the more I appreciate the predictable wind and rain and heat of that tiny corner of the Third World where I grew up.

The worst disruption to this region is caused by rain. Usually just once a year, thankfully. They say that in the old days these terrible downpours used to come only once every ten years, making rivers flood their banks, turning streets into canals, cutting villages off from the rest of the world. Some true *pique-culs* like Jean-Pierre say the fact that it now happens more often is a normal part of an age-old cycle. Nothing to worry about. There have always been these inexplicable shifts in the weather from time to time. For some of the other villagers, like Madame Voisine, it's just more evidence that mankind is destroying the planet.

I haven't lived here long enough to venture an opinion. I'm still an *étrangère*, remember. But in less than two years in our stone house in Church Street, I've watched the river burst its banks twice, flood the *boules* ground and the park and the street in front of the *mairie*, and chase several people from their homes.

One of Alain's colleagues in a neighbouring village lost nearly all her worldly possessions last autumn when more than a metre of water rushed through her house. The government declared a state of emergency and made a huge amount of money available to help people out of their misery, and the insurance company compensated her for her furniture and her carpets and her curtains and her clothes and who knows what else, and after months of suffering, Pierette was finally happy in her house once more.

And then, barely a year later, it started to rain ominously hard once again ...

Poor Pierette's house was flooded for the second time.

We are lucky. We live two streets away from the river. The water doesn't rise this far. Well it did, once – four hundred years ago – and the church across the street was severely damaged by floodwaters. But that's the kind of natural disaster that hits a town once every few centuries. We can only hope that the next one comes only in the next century.

Even so, when the river started to rise that first autumn, I was very anxious. The school principal called and asked parents to fetch their children from school urgently because the playground was being flooded. And Alain called from work to say that he might not be able to get home that night, because several bridges in the area were flooded. And when I walked in the direction of the river – driving was out of the question because the street had already turned into a canal – I was alarmed to see that the park bench where I'd sat just the previous day was no longer visible above the water. And back at home the water was starting to seep underneath the front door. Before long the entire passage was wet and slippery. While the rumble of the rain on the roof kept getting louder.

That was when I thought – seriously, for the first time in my life – of those mental lists you always make of what you'd grab if your house were threatened by a fire or an earthquake or some other disaster. Like a flood, for example. I'd always thought that I'd grab my computer, what else, because that's where all my work of the preceding weeks, months and even years would be stored. Furniture and clothes and books and paintings could all in some sense be replaced, but no insurance company could give me back a manuscript I'd toiled on for three years. That's what I thought. And photographs and letters from people close to me, perhaps even harder to replace than a manuscript, those were the next things I'd grab. A few photo albums, the file where I kept my most precious letters, and what else?

Well, now I know.

That day I realised that I didn't even have enough hands to grab the children and the dog. And that nothing else really mattered. What you grab, when your house is threatened by a disaster, is the living beings around you. Your people and your animals. Those are the only things that are really impossible to replace.

Fortunately it wasn't necessary to grab anything. Unlike the people in many other houses in the village, we got only our feet wet. And Alain came home that night after all, after an incredible detour.

Days later the streets around us were still rumbling with the noise of the pump which the fire brigade used to try and suck up the water.

What amazed me, when it began pouring again a year later and the school sent the children home again and the park bench disappeared beneath the rising river water again, was that this time I wasn't panic-stricken at all. A little irritated, perhaps. Another bloody flood. Maybe even a little blasé.

Now that I think about it, this time I behaved less like an *étrangère*, and more like a true *pique-cul*. More like Jean-Pierre sitting impassively on his bar stool while the street outside turned into a canal. *Bof*, he would say, seasons come and seasons go. Another *pastis*, please. The river rises and the river falls. *Santé*.

It's not as if I want to pretend that I belong here. I know my place. *Étrangère* I was when I came here and *étrangère* I will be when I leave. I just mean that maybe I'm getting used to the rain and snow, wind and lightning.

Up to a point, of course. We Africans are just not designed for extremely cold conditions. That struck me again last week, after two African members of an élite unit in the French army had frozen to death during a kind of survival camp in the Alps. The guys who were born in Europe all survived.

Coincidence? How would I know? I just know that I feel the cold much sooner than my own family's French contingent. The blood of my distant European ancestors no longer flows thickly enough in my veins to protect me from temperatures below freezing.

But just to put the matter in perspective. This morning while I was complaining that the winter seemed particularly harsh this year, I heard on the radio that temperatures dropped to minus 61 degrees Celsius in Quebec, Canada, last night. And minus 25 degrees in New York, where my poor sister is living at the moment. And suddenly I was so relieved about not living in North America that I completely forgot the cold here in France.

20 Don't tempt fate

'I firmly believe that bad luck comes in waves,' a Cape Town friend wrote last week after I'd bemoaned the fate that recently brought a string of afflictions into my hearth and home, 'and your wave has now passed.'

Well, I have news for my optimistic friend. It ain't over till the fat lady sings. And now this woman, who may not be a lady and fortunately also not too fat, will nevertheless sing loudly about all the low blows life can deal you when you're already feeling a little punch drunk. In the hopes that such a public lament will make the wheels of fate turn in another direction for a change.

I've already told you that I'm not superstitious. I don't believe in the Chinese horoscope or the secrets of tea leaves in the bottom of cups. But sometimes I suspect that maybe bad luck does, in some strange magnetic way, attract more bad luck.

Because exactly one day after my friend informed me that my bad-luck wave had passed, my three-year-old daughter drank a few mouthfuls from a bottle of petrol. I know, I know, I can't blame her. The petrol (for a heater) has an innocent transparent colour. It had been poured into an innocent water bottle. Which stood innocently, within easy reach, in the living room.

My only excuse is that neither my better half nor I was fully conscious. We were both suffering from a mild case of shell shock. Because for the past month or so (and especially the last week), life had been particularly trying here in the tranquil French countryside.

Let me put it this way. In winter, outside the tourist season, exactly nothing happens here in Provence. But in our home, winter is apparently the season for drama. Action-packed, heart-rending drama. Blood and injuries and diseases and accidents and howling ambulance sirens. Sometimes I feel as if I am trapped inside one of those generic American TV series about an emergency room in a big hospital. And usually I play the part of the only nurse on duty.

This winter's bad-luck wave began when Alain slipped on the wet pavement outside the local supermarket, knocked himself out and was rushed to hospital in an ambulance. (My friend Michiel claims that it wasn't the rain that made the pavement so slippery. His theory is that any French pavement is hazardous to life because it is so smeared with dog turds.) They kept Alain in hospital a few days to make sure he hadn't sustained concussion or worse. He'd barely come home, when Daniel sprained his ankle at school and spent a week on crutches. In the meantime, Hugo had traded blows with a classmate and was symbolically 'suspended' for a day. (It wasn't fair, he sobbed, the other guy had started the fight! It's always the other guy, as every parent knows.) Daniel had scarcely put away his crutches when Alain had a car accident. Someone rammed into him from behind and he injured his neck and had to wear a neck brace for a week. The car was also quite badly damaged. It is currently at a garage for repairs, a leisurely operation here in Provence, which means that for the next few weeks we'll have to make do with a single unreliable car. Instead of two unreliable cars as usual.

Meanwhile the entire family has succumbed, one by one, to a stomach virus. Everyone stayed in bed for three days, that is, everyone except me who had to remain standing to wipe up vomit and fetch medicine. Well, somebody had to do it.

That is why, on a bleak and cold Monday morning, I

bemoaned my fate via e-mail. And then I got the encouraging message from my Cape Town friend. And then my daughter decided to drink petrol, just to make sure that our lives didn't become too dull.

While Mia screamed to raise the roof about the awful taste in her mouth, and I tried to shove my finger down her throat, Alain called the emergency poison line. I vaguely remembered Daniel swallowing paraffin while we still lived in South Africa, and being told by someone at a similar emergency number to give him milk. But Mia flatly refused to take a single sip of milk. She just screamed LOUDER.

Meanwhile the anonymous voice at the emergency number managed to ease our minds a little. A few mouthfuls of petrol weren't fatal, it seemed. But just as I was heaving a big sigh of relief, the voice warned us that some children did develop breathing problems after such an exotic drink. We were therefore cautioned to watch our daughter closely and to take her to hospital the minute it looked as if she was struggling to breathe.

She was so exhausted from her ear-splitting screaming that she was asleep within half an hour. I would have liked to say that I didn't sleep a wink the entire night. That I kept checking if my daughter was still breathing properly, the way every dutiful mother would.

But I was so exhausted myself, after a week of endless nights with vomiting children, that I slept like a baby. I didn't wake up until Alain leaped out of bed early in the morning and staggered to the bathroom because he hadn't got rid of his stomach bug yet.

And then I remembered my Cape Town friend's optimistic words of comfort. And I realised that this winter's bad-luck wave had, alas, not passed.

And yet we've survived worse winters. Three years ago the 'quiet season' began for me with an orthodontic operation that went wrong. It caused a disgusting infection in my mouth and led to weeks of pain and suffering. I had to swallow drawers full of pills and antibiotics and at one stage I had to pay a string of nurses to come and give me an injection in my backside every day.

The worst was that I couldn't eat properly. If there is one thing that breaks my spirit, it is not being allowed to eat what I want.

No, the absolute worst was that I put on weight – despite assurances from several friends that the only possible advantage of a painful mouth was that one would surely lose a kilo or two. Don't ask me how I managed to emerge heavier at the other end. Maybe it's just because self-pity is such a heavy load to carry.

Then one morning while I was still struggling with my mouth, I discovered that I was virtually blind in one eye. I was lying snugly behind my beloved's back, and aiming with my right eye over his shoulder at the framed family photo next to the bed – and then I realised with an ice-cold shock that I could not see the family photo. Everything was a blur. When I closed my left eye, even my beloved's shoulder right under my nose became a blurry mass.

We got an urgent appointment at the optometrist (which borders on a miracle around here) and later the same day we were told that I had grown a cataract on my right eye. For the second time in two years. Which is extremely rare, according to the optometrist, at my youthful age. I was so buoyed up by being called youthful – when did *that* last happen? – that I almost forgot to panic over the fact that I had to undergo another operation.

If you're hovering around your fortieth birthday, developing a cataract is not such a bad idea. You may feel middle-aged and miserable, but suddenly the medical fraternity treats you like a sort of child prodigy. Someone who has been able to do what only older people – much older people – usually manage.

But even my restored youth (in the eyes of my optometrist, at any rate) couldn't really make me look forward to a second eye operation. Cataracts are removed with laser beams, not a painful process at all, but it's rather gruesome having your bare eyeball worked on while you're completely conscious. You see the most incredible colours and psychedelic patterns spatter before you.

Probably the closest I'll ever come to an LSD trip, I thought during the first operation. Interesting, having such an imitation drug experience, without all the drawbacks of real drugs. But once is enough.

In the end the second laser operation was a less serious business. In the first operation a kind of imitation lens is transplanted onto your eyeball, which makes it easier to remove future cataracts. Because a cataract, I've discovered in the meantime, is a cat with nine lives. The reason most cataract patients don't undergo repeat operations is quite simply that most of them are already so old that they die before they can be operated on again.

But my optometrist didn't deign to explain these things to me before the second operation. Medical people are inclined to treat you like an idiot if you struggle to speak their language. And while I was waiting with growing fear for the day of the operation, I went for my annual routine visit to the gynaecologist – and discovered that there was 'strange tissue' present in my breasts.

What next? I asked out loud. First my mouth, then my eye, now my breasts. Would it be my ears next week?

It probably wasn't malignant, the gynaecologist immediately tried to comfort me, but it had to be watched.

A few months later I would hear that it was a false alarm – but that day I got such a fright that I sent an SOS into cyberspace. To inform those near and dear to me via the Internet that I was fed up with all these physical afflictions. And suddenly I made a fascinating discovery.

If it is true that bad luck and illness attract more bad luck and illness – and of course I still hope that it is just my imagination – then it is also true that bad-luck stories attract bad-luck stories. A case of I show you mine (my misfortune, that is), then you show me yours. That same day (and the next, and the next) I was swamped by complaints from my friends who I had thought were much more fortunate than me. From relationship problems to medical problems, from financial crises to existential crises, you name them, my friends had them. I never dreamt the pour souls were struggling so. Thought I was the only poor wretch among us.

'It's our age,' Louisa wrote from London. 'We are all approaching middle age. It's the beginning of the end.'

And that's supposed to make me feel better?

No, my husband said in his rational way, our struggles had nothing to do with age. (Because in the meantime a wave of adversity had knocked him off his feet as well.) After all, my orthodontic problems were merely the result of a wisdom tooth that was supposed to have made its appearance twenty years earlier, but had worked underground all these years like a sly terrorist and caused an uprising among the other teeth. (If all this suffering sounds vaguely familiar, please read the postscript at the end of this chapter.) And my eye trouble had arrived about thirty years too early. And the 'strange tissue', well, that could happen to a teenager too.

And the fact that my husband became deaf overnight, that can also not be attributed to age. No, that's probably my fault. I tempted fate. That day at the gynaecologist when I asked what was next. My ears?

Then it turned out to be my husband's ears.

Because a few days later, I kid you not, Alain succumbed to a strange virus that caused an unbearable buzzing in his left ear. By the weekend he had lost eighty percent of his hearing in that ear. Then he had to spend a week in hospital and a few hours every day in a kind of oxygen tank, a mask on his face, like a deep-sea diver. And receive cortisone treatment that made his cheeks swell up and other medication that gave him palpitations, and I was consumed by guilt.

Never again would I make sarcastic remarks about medical problems.

The fringe benefit of the oxygen tank was that it made the cut on Alain's hand heal faster.

Because in the interim our hearth and home had been hit by another horrible accident. Alain was washing the dishes (which were piled up to the ceiling because we spent all our available hours in doctors' waiting rooms) when an enormous porcelain bowl 'exploded' in his hands. That's how he explained it to me a few seconds later, pale with shock. The back of his hand and at least one finger were cut open to the bone. I wanted to faint when I saw the bloody mess, but I had a baby on the hip and couldn't fall without hurting the baby, so I stayed standing.

Another example of an accident that could hit anyone at any age. It's just that I couldn't figure out why it had to hit *us* and why it had to hit us *now*. Between the two of us we now had an infected mouth, an almost blind eye, a pair of distressing breasts, a deaf ear and an injured hand. And the baby on my hip had bronchitis.

Impossible as it may seem, that winter's bad-luck wave was still not over. A week later I missed the train on the way to a very important meeting with a publisher in Paris. I tried to stay calm, because there was after all still the slow night train that could deliver me to the banks of the Seine at the crack of dawn the next morning. All the sleeping compartments were already occupied, which meant that I had to sleep sitting up in an ordinary carriage. Rather uncomfortable but not the end of the world.

Then came the end of the world.

In the middle of the night my purse was stolen from my handbag. From underneath my head, as it were, because like any experienced traveller I kept my possessions close to my body, and had been using my handbag as a pillow. I still cannot explain how it happened. I am armed with the common South African suspicion of my fellow man, but in all my travels nothing like this had ever happened to me.

It just goes to show, I thought while I sat in the grey morning light on a station bench in Paris, as broke as the bearded tramp next to me. I didn't know exactly what this experience was supposed to show me – but maybe it had something to do with the Chinese horoscope after all? When the tramp asked me for money, I burst into tears. I didn't have a *centime* to my name. I didn't have a bankcard or a credit card. I couldn't even buy a cup of coffee to drive away the cold and the self-pity.

The tramp jumped up in fright and fled.

When things go wrong, they really *go wrong*, as Godley and Crème used to sing. *And they rarely go right for meee* ... Alain often sings this song at home. Especially during the Provençal winter. We know the sun will shine again, the lavender will bloom again, the vineyards turn green again. And we know that our bad-luck wave will pass.

Or rather, we hope that our current bad-luck wave will also pass.

Postscript

While we were struggling with our health that winter, I was writing a novel. Usually at night, because during the day we were usually at doctors and hospitals. And then one night I decided, no way. Such pain can't be in vain. If I couldn't find a reason for so much suffering, then I could at least try to find a purpose for it.

And that's how it came about that the main character in the novel, *Travelling Light*, was struck by a series of physical disasters. Teeth, eyes, ears, you name it. I changed the details of some of the complaints, but kept the broad outline.

Some readers probably thought that it was a bit thick. How on earth could a healthy woman be afflicted with so many ailments in such a short time?

That's what I also want to know.

In my life truth is often stranger than fiction.

21   The kissing won't stop

The French have many habits which visiting friends and relatives find surprising. Like the fact that the cheese board appears on the table before dessert. First you eat the cheese, and then something sweet to round off the meal. Or the fact that a plate of green salad leaves is considered a separate dish, to be eaten before or after the main course, but never, ever with the main course.

Or take a French braai, for example. No thanks, my cousin would say, the French can keep that for themselves. Six emaciated little sausages for six people is a bloody insult to the word 'braai'. And then to top it all, these skinny sausages burn your mouth!

It's true that the reddish *merguez* sausages have quite a bite. In our family even the children love them. But when South African friends visit, we would rather braai chipolatas. They're as skinny as *merguez*, but more brown than red, in other words stuffed with fewer spices. Or the fat sausage of Toulouse, the closest we get to boerewors here, in appearance at any rate. We'll keep quiet about the taste. Boerewors is boerewors, as most of my male relatives maintain, and French sausage is sissy sausage.

When we have a braai here, we're really just looking for an excuse to make a little fire, not to eat outside, because that we do every day anyway, two or three times a day, throughout summer.

While in South Africa, as I recall, we cook the meat outside but often eat it inside. Because it's too hot outside or because the insects are a pest or because the only comfortable table is inside the house.

In South Africa, I still suspect, a braai is chiefly an excuse for the men to get away from the women, to tell dirty jokes and analyse the weekend's rugby game minute by minute, while the other sex stays behind in the kitchen to make potato salad and jabber about such utter trifles as the children's education.

Here the emphasis is on the braai rather than on the meat. It's okay if there are only six little sausages on the grid, because there are always more than enough side dishes. Starters and in-between courses, salads and vegetables, olives and cheese. No one is going to go hungry. Except perhaps my cousin who believes that food without meat isn't really food. When my cousin and his mates have a braai, you can easily expect four different kinds of meat on your plate – boerewors, mutton chops, ribs and steak – with one enormous potato on the side.

Here things are different. And I don't just mean food and eating habits. But while we are busy with matters of the mouth: if there is one thing that strikes more terror in the heart of the average South African man than a plate with too little meat on it, it is having to kiss another man. And here in France the men are always kissing each other.

Not just the men, of course. Kissing is a national pastime for all sexes and all ages. Most of the time I quite enjoy it. There is something comforting about actually touching your neighbours and your friends and your friends' friends on a daily basis, skin on skin, cheek against cheek. Of course I'm not talking about mouth-to-mouth kisses. These are only, as is proper, employed in the most intimate relationships. I'm talking about the famous French peck on the cheek.

As with any traditional pastime, this one also has different rules in different regions. In Paris you touch each cheek just once. Here in the warm south, you do it three times. Left, right, left. Or right, left, right. The fact that I never know which side to aim for first, left or right, has led to a few ridiculous collisions with neighbours' noses.

And yet this fickleness also strikes me as typical of the French. If the British had been such fanatical cheek kissers, they would long ago have stipulated which side you're supposed to start with. Just think of the escalators in London underground stations. Any Briton knows that you keep right if you want to stand still and left if you want to walk. It's only tourists who bugger up the system. The British are good at making such practical rules to make life simpler. The French evidently are not.

And don't even try to make sense of the rules that do exist. Like exactly how many times in which region you're supposed to touch your neighbour's cheek. At first I thought it was done three times here in the south because people here had more time than the busy Parisians. Or simply because they're more Mediterranean in character, more demonstrative and emotional. Then I discovered that in the area of Lille, where Alain was born, it is done four times. Lille is a big city, full of busy people, and it lies even further to the north than Paris. All the reasons I'd concocted for the threefold kissing action in the south fell flat there and then.

Now I no longer look for reasons. *C'est comme ça*, I tell myself. That's just the way it is.

I'm starting to sound like Jean-Pierre.

All you have to remember is in which part of the country you are when you have to kiss someone, in order to administer the appropriate number of kisses. Because kiss you will. There's no getting round it.

Although I have to admit that I do sometimes try to shirk my duty.

If we arrive at a party and I have to kiss fifteen of Alain's colleagues, plus each one's companion, plus everyone's children – *three* times each – then we're talking about a significant number of kisses. Enough to make you feel exhausted before you even start. Sometimes I get the impression at these social events that I spend the first half of the evening kissing new arrivals – and the second half kissing departing guests. That doesn't leave much time for conversation. That's why I sometimes sneak away from a party like the proverbial thief in the night. Unforgivable, probably. But I am after all a foreigner, and foreigners sometimes do strange things.

If I walk into the local supermarket to buy a packet of coffee and there are five acquaintances in the queue who each have to be kissed three times, then I also sometimes act the foreigner. Just wave my hand through the air in an informal American style and smile into the crowd. For all I know this is also quite unforgivable.

But there are times when you cannot escape the ubiquitous kissing. When you walk into the bar, for instance, and Jean-Pierre is there – and after all he's always there – looking like a dog waiting for his bowl of food until you've kissed him. If you're a woman, that is. He doesn't look at Alain with the same doggy eyes.

And there are times when even South African family and friends are going to be swamped with French kisses. My father turned quite pale with shock when his French son-in-law embraced and kissed him the first time they met. Kissed him *three* times.

'What did I do wrong?' Alain asked me later that evening, concerned.

'I think my father thinks I've married a fairy,' I explained. 'Because of the kissing.'

At that stage Alain had never been to South Africa. He didn't know that South African heterosexual men didn't really kiss other men. I cautioned him to greet my male relatives with a handshake in future.

But my father got over the shock surprisingly quickly. Adapting to changing circumstances was apparently something South African men were getting used to. When my father walked into the kitchen the next morning, Alain did as he'd been told and offered a formal handshake, but this time it was my father who fell around his son-in-law's neck, almost lifting him off his feet in the process, and kissed him enthusiastically. Kissed him *three* times. Over the next few days these two kissed so often I couldn't believe my eyes.

'Either your father is a very good actor,' Alain told me on the day of my father's departure, 'or he's learned to enjoy the kissing quite a bit.'

My personal theory is that most men actually enjoy being embraced by other men. What is a rugby scrum if not a very primitive male embrace? Not to mention the soccer players who leap into each other's arms every time a goal is scored. But I know I would struggle to convince my uncle, my brother or my cousin of this.

I therefore drilled my French husband thoroughly when he came with me to South Africa for the first time, a few months after meeting my dad. Put out your hand. It's okay to touch other men's hands. It's not okay to touch their faces. Palm on palm is no problem. Cheek to cheek is a problem.

In short: Don't kiss anyone who looks as if he doesn't want to be kissed!

He was very obedient. For two weeks he behaved like an anal retentive Calvinist. Wasn't himself at all.

Back in France he started hugging and kissing left, right and centre again with visible relief.

These days I no longer try to change him. But sometimes I wonder if I shouldn't stick a sign onto the gate, the way people do to warn visitors about vicious dogs: *Beware of the kissing man*.

Just so South African visitors will know what to expect.

How long, I once asked a South African woman who'd lived in France for two decades, how long did it take before you could speak French properly?

'But she still can't speak French properly!' her (French) husband shouted indignantly.

It was true, she admitted without hesitation. At the moment, for example, she was going through a strange regression that made her systematically feminise all masculine articles. Change every *le* into a *la*.

'The undermining of male authority?' I speculated hopefully. 'A subconscious declaration of feminism?'

Alas no, she sighed. Because she was also doing it the other way round. Transforming all feminine words into masculine ones.

This conversation made me feel a lot better about my own constant language errors. After all I haven't even been in the country ten years. How could anyone expect me to know the difference between *le* and *la*?

I sometimes manage to convince myself that I am engaged in an anarchistic rebellion against the rigid rules of the Gallic language. Why must every body part, every piece of furniture, every emotion be separated according to gender? Surely it's a form of discrimination? In this era when gender is hardly supposed to matter?

But I've yet to convince a single French citizen of my revolutionary theory.

The problem is, well, that for them it isn't a problem. If you've been speaking French all your life, then you seem to know intuitively that a chair is feminine and a bed masculine. *La chaise* and *le lit*. You don't ask why, you don't look for a logical reason, you just know it. *C'est comme ca*. That's just the way it is.

But if you come to live here only in the second half of your life, then you've got a big problem. *Un grand problème*, says my know-it-all son, not *une grande problème*. But *why*, I ask. Why is a problem always masculine? Then my son rolls his eyes to the ceiling and spreads his palms as if he's checking for rain. (He has acquired several irritating Gallic gestures since we first came to live here.)

'But you can *hear* it's *le problème*, Mom! Surely you can hear that *la problème* doesn't sound right!"

No, my son. I can't hear it. There must be something wrong with my ears.

Easy for him to talk. He was four years old when we got here. At that age children are sponges. They simply absorb any foreign language like water.

I lost my sponginess long ago. Even at high school when the language of Voltaire and Camus first enchanted me, I felt more like a duck than a sponge. The declensions of irregular verbs flowed off my back like water.

And yet I must have had a premonition that one day I'd need this language badly. When in my penultimate school year I ended up at a rural school and heard that French was not taught there, I was actually stubborn enough to continue studying it on my own. As an official seventh subject for my matric exam, with no teacher or mentor or any French-speaking adult to save me from my ignorance.

There was, miracle upon miracle, another pupil who'd lived in

France for a while. A diplomat's daughter if I remember correctly. Her sophisticated European style of dress – a few good pieces instead of dozens of cheap dresses like the rest of us – was a revelation that confounded us rural boarders. I asked her advice whenever I got stuck with my French lessons. Even tried out a few jerky French sentences on her sometimes.

But most of the time I felt like someone who was taking swimming lessons in the middle of the Sahara. My knowledge was purely theoretical. If you had to toss me into a French conversation, I'd have sunk like a stone.

Two decades later when I settled in the French countryside, the situation had changed completely. By then I had long lost my theoretical knowledge, all rusted away in the twenty years during which it lay unused at the back of my mind, but suddenly I was in a place where no one spoke anything but French. I had to sink or swim. Speak – however imperfectly – or perish.

Before I arrived I was warned that the rural French 'didn't really' speak English. I didn't realise that meant they spoke no English at all. Jean-Pierre, for example, knows precisely three phrases in English. 'Do you want to sleep with me?' (With the requisite charming French accent of course.) If the woman says no, she doesn't want to sleep with him, he says, 'No problem.' If she agrees, he says, 'Thank you very much.' That's the sum of Jean-Pierre's English.

And that is considerably more than some of the other villagers can manage.

So I started to swim, a feeble doggy style that I had to make up as I went along, a little rusty theory mixed with a whole lot of improvisation. I'm still swimming. My head no longer disappears below the water every few minutes, which probably means that I'm making progress, but I sometimes wonder if I'll ever feel solid ground beneath my feet.

Ever since hearing about my friend's strange regression with the gender of words, I suspect that I will flounder around in the French language for the rest of my life, from one error to the next, from *la problème* to *le catastrophe*, always attaching the wrong gender to the wrong word.

My only consolation in these humiliating circumstances is that I didn't go to live in Germany. There I would have been floundering among three genders. The masculine *der*, the feminine *die* and that pesky little transvestite of a *das*.

And I often thank the gods, the stars and other heavenly bodies that French is such a mumbling sort of language. The words have a way of running into each other, the final syllable mostly disappearing in your mouth, the final letter usually as superfluous as an appendix. It makes it possible to cheat. To deliberately mumble *leah* if you're not sure if it's *le* or *la*. Like in those monkey puzzle exams where you draw your cross more or less halfway between the 'yes' and 'no' to cover every possible answer. Often it doesn't work, because the gender of one word can also bedevil several others, but sometimes it does work. And that's all any cheat – in a language or an exam – can hope for.

Apparently the French find it quite cute when Anglo-Saxon stars such as Jane Birkin or Charlotte Rampling make blatant language errors. But I'm no Birkin or Rampling. I never get the impression that anyone in my little village considers my imperfect French 'cute'. Usually they just smile patiently – as when you listen to a feeble-minded person or a stammerer – while I struggle to say my piece. I sometimes expect Madame Voisine to offer me a dog biscuit because I try so tail-waggingly hard. But she would undoubtedly prefer it, as would the other villagers, if I learnt to speak the language properly.

Now that I've sketched the background, you will understand my horror when a French publisher called to ask if I felt up to taking part in a literary TV programme. And not just any programme. France is probably the only country in the world where an erudite programme about books and authors was among the most popular programmes on TV for fifteen years. (Or perhaps it just says something about the rest of the stuff on TV.) By the time I came to live here, Bernard Pivot's famous *Apostrophes* had been replaced with a broader cultural programme that also covered theatre and art and so on. But the presenter was still the formidable Monsieur Pivot, regarded by many French as a sort of unofficial minister of culture, and the programme was everything but a soapie. Certainly not what you'd call 'easy viewing'.

I therefore didn't hesitate for a moment. I wasn't up to it, I answered, terrified. Absolutely not.

But the French publisher, who'd just published a translation of my first adult novel, took a different view.

'Just think of the incredible publicity!' she cried.

'Just think of the incredible humiliation!' I cried. 'Every time I try to say something, I'll sound like the village idiot of the French countryside!'

There, there, the publisher soothed, it won't be that hard. All I had to do was work out a few answers beforehand, and then ask my husband or another Frenchman to correct the grammar, and then learn the corrected version off by heart, and then just rattle off these answers. Never mind what questions I was asked.

But surely my answers should have *some* vague connection with the questions?

Nothing to worry about, my confident publisher assured me. After all, they always asked the same sort of questions in this kind of programme. Something about feminism, something about autobiographical elements in your work, something about your previous or your next book …

No, I said. Even in Afrikaans or English I struggled to talk about my own work. To do it in imperfect French, on national TV, while my son's teacher rolled her eyes to the ceiling and wondered how such an intelligent child could possibly have such an idiotic mother …

No way.

Well, nothing had been arranged, the publisher tried to placate me. She'd just wanted to test my reaction. Think about it, she said encouragingly. We'd talk soon.

It wasn't necessary to think about it. I knew that many French writers would pawn their computers and their friends for a chance to take part in such a programme. But I wasn't a French writer. I was an Afrikaans writer battling to speak French.

The only problem was convincing my publisher – without contradicting her so much that she'd refuse to publish my next book – that not all publicity was good publicity. That sometimes it was better for a writer to keep her mouth shut and let her book speak on her behalf.

And then my doctor saved me. I was pregnant with Mia, who was suddenly threatening to put in an early appearance (because I was so stressed over the stupid TV programme, for all I knew), so the doctor ordered me to move as little as possible. I'd never been so grateful for a ban on my personal movements. It meant that I couldn't possibly undertake the long journey to Paris to take part in a literary TV programme.

So I never had my fifteen minutes of fame (or shame or scandal) on French television. And the publisher did indeed refuse to buy my next book. The first one had apparently not sold as well as she had hoped – but I believe to this day that the book would've fared a lot worse if I'd tried to peddle it on TV.

Now that I've lived here a few years more, I've actually become brave enough to occasionally address high-school pupils or students in the area about South African writers. Well, the idea is that I have to talk about writers, but my audience generally knows so little about South Africa that I have to start with a geography lesson. I first have to point out on a map of the world where this unknown little country is, then quickly tell them something about the climate and vegetation, the various population groups and many languages and so on – before I switch to a very basic history lesson. More than three centuries of wars and uprisings and political intrigue summarised in a few paragraphs. If I talk really fast (which in French I'm still not able to do), there's usually half an hour left after the geographical and historical introduction to cover South African literature in its entirety.

Let me give you an example of the level of ignorance. When I first went to talk at the *lycée* in Orange, one of the pupils was under the impression that I was Karen Blixen. Apparently the only female writer 'out of Africa' she'd ever heard of (and probably only because of the movie starring Meryl Streep). I tried to explain that the writer of *Out of Africa* (a) wasn't born in Africa and (b) was no longer alive – but I'm not sure that she (a) understood me and (b) believed me.

Why do I do it? I'm not sure. I would like to say that it's a kind of missionary zeal to spread the glad tidings about my country's literature. But if I'm totally honest I have to admit that it's probably just another attempt to improve my dreadful French. It rounds off my social skills a little. It makes small talk with my husband's colleagues a little easier.

Put another way, the next time I find myself at one of those long dining tables and someone dares to ask me about my country of origin, I can bore my poor table companion to death with an extensive lecture that ranges from the population groups in my country to the literature of my country.

I have even risked talking on radio. All right, it was just once and it was really just a high-school radio station, so I don't suppose it really counts. But for me it was a Big Leap on my long journey towards self-confidence in the Gallic language.

Although I probably switched my genders and made a mess of my irregular verbs, I could at least understand what the teenaged interviewers were asking me. And that's harder than you may think.

Just ask any South African soul who's had to do this.

Louis the Painter, who lives in a magnificent château in the Limousin, gave me an embarrassed account of his first radio interview in French. All very informal, he just had to chat a little about his career as an artist, right there at his kitchen table. But when the woman turned on her tape recorder and asked the first question, he became deaf. His brain got stuck, his tongue knotted, his lungs collapsed. He couldn't understand a word she was saying. Nothing. And yet he could swear that moments earlier he hadn't had this strange comprehension problem.

So he said 'Pardon?' And she repeated the question. And still he understood nothing. After she'd asked the question for the third time, he couldn't say pardon again without sounding deaf or mentally disabled. So he just went blah-blah. Started to chirp like a cheerful bird without having the faintest idea what the question had been about.

He struggled throughout the entire interview in this way. After the programme was broadcast, a local resident assured him that she'd understood his every word. The only thing she didn't understand, she told him with a puzzled frown, was why he'd refused to answer any of the interviewer's questions.

As an unexpected consequence of one of my high-school talks about South Africa's climate and vegetation, a journalist from our regional paper came to interview me. Just to avoid any misunderstanding, we're not talking about *Le Monde*. Our regional paper is like those old-fashioned country newspapers in South Africa. Every village gets half a page for 'news' about births, school concerts and outings for the old-age home. The reports are usually written by local correspondents who use too many adjectives. And the pictures are nearly always out of focus.

But my picture was actually in focus. The journalist was a full-time reporter, not a farmer's wife who covered the village's weddings and funerals in-between her other tasks. There were about five factual errors in fifteen lines, unfortunately – but I was quite prepared to blame my bad French rather than the journalist's bad journalism for that.

The bonus was that for the first time Mia's teacher – and probably not a few of her classmates' mothers – believed that I actually worked. Up until then the teacher had looked askance every time she and her colleagues went on strike (which happened quite often), and only 'working parents' had the right to leave their children in the school crèche. As if I were just a lazy mother who wanted to get rid of her children so she could watch TV all day long.

It's true that I don't look terribly professional when I arrive at the school gate in the mornings in my tracksuit pants with uncombed hair. I should probably have tried to explain to the teacher that my kind of work didn't require power dressing. On the contrary. Writing, like yoga, seems less difficult when you're comfortably dressed. And why would I brush my hair and make up my face if my only company was going to be a few characters in a book-in-progress?

I probably should've tried. *Le problème* was that I found it too difficult to explain this sort of thing in French. I preferred to keep quiet and be thought of as a lazy TV-addict.

So the newspaper interview did bring me a little respect at the school gate. The other mothers didn't exactly rush up to beg for my autograph. But for at least a few weeks I shed my reputation as the laziest mother in the village.

And then the school year ended. And Mia got a new teacher. And this new teacher looks at me askance, believe it or not, every time there is a teachers' strike (which still happens quite often), and I use my 'work' as an excuse for leaving my child at the crèche …

23 Camping is no picnic

Quite early in our relationship Alain extracted from me a solemn promise that we would never go camping. And just because friends from Cambridge had brought their caravan to a local camping site and we helped them pitch their tent alongside it. Or rather, we tried to help, but we got so entangled in the ropes and poles that we ended up crawling on the ground, helpless with laughter. We clearly lacked the aptitude for such complicated matters as camping.

But early in a relationship one makes many promises. A few years later, when we were beginning to grasp the full catastrophe of our large family, we realised that camping was the only way we'd ever be able to afford a decent holiday. Did I say *decent*? Correction. A camping holiday is by its very nature not decent. At least not our sort of camping holiday.

We have too many children and not enough 'equipment'. We don't have a luxury caravan or an impressive camping vehicle equipped with power points and a toilet and a sink and an oven and a fridge. All we have are a few small, primitive tents and inflatable mattresses, a collection of torches as our only light source, a sturdy cool box and a small gas stove. And during our last (and, believe me, our last ever) camping holiday, my husband forgot the gas stove and several other essential items at home.

Further correction. A camping holiday isn't really a holiday at all. It's an oxymoron. You cannot camp and be on holiday in the same breath. At least I can't. I don't have enough breath left for being on holiday while I'm taking care of a family of six with no modern conveniences.

A year or three ago I decided the time was ripe to introduce my own personal French legion to Africa. Or to that corner of Africa at any rate where my own roots were. After we'd paid for six plane tickets, there wasn't much of a budget left for the month we wanted to spend travelling through South Africa and Namibia. Hotels and guesthouses were out of the question. So for the most part was the hospitality of family and friends, simply because there were so many of us. (In tribute to my family and friends I should mention that many of them offered to accommodate the whole lot of us, but in most cases it was simply not practical.) A camping trip was our only option.

We borrowed my father's camping vehicle, attached a trailer which we loaded with tents and ropes and sleeping bags and braai equipment, and ventured into Africa's wide-open spaces. For the Frenchmen among us the trip was an absolute revelation. Alain learnt to build a fire that would've made any Voortrekker proud. A mother of a fire with coals that glowed throughout the dark night so that you could boil your coffee water on it early the next morning. Thomas the City Teenager learnt to endure flies and gnats and other insects (after complaining non-stop for the first few days) and to pee in the great outdoors (something else that initially made him moan and groan). Hugo learnt to walk barefoot all day long and go to bed with disgustingly dirty feet at night.

Mia, then barely eighteen months old, learnt to scare us all to death by vanishing without a trace whenever we were pitching tents and stoking the cooking fire. In Namaqualand we thought she'd been carried off by baboons. In the Etosha Game Reserve we thought she'd been carried off by lions. Somebody would notice that the baby had disappeared and immediately raise the alarm. Then the entire family would scatter panic-stricken in every direction to try to rescue her from the claws of wild animals.

Time and again we found her in other campers' tents. Where she had made herself at home uninvited and was trying to seduce bewildered strangers with a unique baby language made up of smatterings of Afrikaans, French and something that sounded Japanese. I noticed that all the tents she ran away to were less primitive than ours, and suspected that she (like her mother) would've preferred more luxurious accommodation.

When I shared my theory with Alain, he pointed out that *all* the other tents were less primitive than ours.

What amazed me most about this 'holiday' was that the different members of our family had such different memories of it afterwards. Mia was too young and I usually too tired to remember anything. Aside from the search parties for the lost baby and the enormous bundles of washing I had to scrub by hand. While Alain and the three boys still get excited about the elephants of Etosha, the majestic sand dunes of the Namib Desert, the early-morning swim in the steaming hot spring water of Ai-Ais, the magnificent wild flowers of Namaqualand, the endless white beach at Stilbaai, the romping whales right outside the harbour wall at Hermanus ...

Where was I during all these unforgettable experiences?

My body was there, I'm told, but my spirit was constantly engaged with the logistical nightmare of such a travelling circus. How to get our hands on enough food. How to get the food cooked. How to get the pots clean ...

And then I actually did it again. Here in Europe a camping holiday would surely be different from one in the uncivilised conditions of Africa! That's what I told myself before the family went camping in France last year.

Our destination was one of the most scenic parts of scenic

Brittany. Quaint stone cottages on towering cliffs high above the sea, gigantic shrubs covered in purple-blue hydrangea wherever you looked, Celtic music and old women in traditional garb with strange headdresses resembling wrapped-up toilet rolls.

Magnifique, said Madame Voisine, clasping her birdlike claws in ecstasy. When Monsieur was still well, they went camping in Bretagne sometimes. Monsieur was never a very enthusiastic camper, she owned – and for the first time I felt a hint of empathy with her invisible husband – but she always loved it. I could imagine. Doing your laundry in a communal basin in a camping site is probably as close as you can get to a convivial washday at the communal *lavoir* in a Provençal village of long ago.

Personally I prefer to do my laundry in the privacy of my own home. Just another reason why I, like Monsieur, will never be an enthusiastic camper.

En route to our destination in Brittany we planned to stay overnight in the regions of the Lozère and Auvergne. We were going to take it easy, plan our route carefully, no mad rush to reach the next isolated hamlet by sunrise. Unlike in Africa.

In France, even the simplest camping sites usually have at least a washing machine and a tumble dryer. And a café where you can buy the newspaper and a fresh croissant every morning. And if there is no supermarket on the site itself, you're bound to find a few shops within a few kilometres with everything your heart desires. In France nothing is ever more than a few kilometres away.

That's what I kept telling myself. Because one of the few things I do remember about our camping trip in Africa is the panic that hit us when, somewhere on the godforsaken plains of Namibia, Mia suddenly developed a dangerously high fever. And we could tell from the map that we were 200 km away from the nearest town with a doctor or pharmacy.

In France something like this would never happen, I assured Alain while we packed.

Well, now I know.

Camping in France is entirely different from camping in Africa. But it is still a nightmare.

It's true that in France you don't have to fear that a baboon or a lion will carry off your child. And the flies aren't half as troublesome as in Africa. And you never have to pee out of doors because the distance to the nearest toilet is never greater than the capacity of your bladder.

But for the first three nights, sky-high in the mountains of the Lozère, we were attacked by the most determined mosquitoes I've ever come across in my life. And I know mosquitoes. I spent part of my childhood in the old Transvaal Lowveld. But these French *moustiques* took no notice of the usual deterrents. We lit a wide variety of special candles and coils. We covered ourselves from head to toe in stinking ointments and sprayed ourselves with cans of even stinkier prophylactics. We were nevertheless covered in mosquito bites every morning. By day three the boys began to look as if they had smallpox. They refused to wear their swimming costumes in public.

So we packed our tents and our meagre equipment onto the roof of our station wagon and fled to our next camping site with our tails between our legs. Driven away by mosquitoes. A bitter defeat for a woman out of Africa.

In the Auvergne there were no mosquitoes. But nor was there the cool mountain air of the Lozère which had protected us from the worst heat wave to hit France in decades. I'm talking about the sort of heat that would've been difficult to handle even in a house with air-conditioning. In two tiny tents with just one scanty tree nearby – all the shady spots had of course been taken – the heat was dangerous. (It's the very same heat wave in which thousands of elderly French would die, although no one knew it at the time.) I would've loved to pack up and go home – but we'd let our house (with air-conditioning in my bedroom!) to friends of friends for two weeks.

Our only survival tactic was getting up at dawn, eating breakfast while it was still half-dark, and making sure that we were at the swimming pool complex next door as soon as the gate opened. Then we spent the rest of the day in or beside the water. We saw none of the famous attractions of the Auvergne region. Just this swimming pool complex, which wasn't mentioned in any tourist brochure.

It was in the Auvergne that I discovered that my husband the daydreamer had left our camping table, our only camping chair, our braai grid and our gas stove at home. See, in the mountains of the Lozère we'd camped next to a holiday house belonging to friends. We'd cooked and eaten our food inside the house. Sounds like cheating, I know, but we needed that bit of civilisation. The rest of our 'holiday' would be truly barbaric.

In the Auvergne, because of my husband's unforgivable forget-fulness, we had to eat sitting flat on the ground while ants and other insects crawled over our tin plates. Our menu consisted of sandwiches and more sandwiches. Or else something that could be cooked outside over the fire. But without a grid. With sticks and other primitive tools.

Even my indispensable cup of morning coffee was the cause of a whole lot of trouble. Because the café wasn't yet open (I said we had to get up really early), Alain boiled the water on a fire. The way he'd been taught in Africa.

With one important difference, namely that we were now in the heart of Europe. No European camper has apparently ever seen anyone make a fire to boil water for coffee. On the first morning a group of children who were up early formed a curious little circle around him while he tried to stoke the flame with slow puffs. By the next morning the rumour about this strange behavi-our had spread through the camping site. This time a few of the children's daddies joined the little circle.

I sulked while I waited for my coffee, still angry with my hus-band for leaving an entire box of important camping equipment behind, and considered whether we could charge admission to this open-air concert. Maybe then we could afford to buy a gas stove and a grid.

Later that day I went and bought a gas stove and a grid anyway.

And when at last we arrived in Brittany, we discovered that the camping site had no fireplaces at all. All the other campers had brought along magnificent portable braais – or cooked their food on the super modern stoves inside their super modern caravans. It was only our lot who were stupid enough to think that a cosy fire was an indispensable part of any outdoor holiday.

By the end of this European camping trip my heart ached with longing for Africa. For primitive camping sites where you can make a fire right there on the ground and listen to the night sounds of insects or wild animals, instead of the bleating radios and boring arguments of other campers all around you. For camping sites where you can see the stars at night instead of bright street lights and the gas lamps of hundreds of caravans. For camping sites, in short, where you're not so swamped by crowds of Europeans that you get claustrophobic palpitations. Give me the godforsaken plains of Africa!

The omnipresence of nothing, as Thomas remarked in a philosophical moment somewhere in the Namib Desert.

Now that I think about it, I never heard Thomas say anything philosophical throughout our camping trip in Europe. Which in itself probably says something about the whole experience.

24   Where the heart is

The heart of our home has got to be the kitchen. Just as life-giving blood is pumped to the furthest extremities of the body to keep the entire organism going, so food and drink is constantly carried from our kitchen to the remotest corners of our home.

The coffee and rusks which my husband brings me in bed in the morning, the clandestine snacks the children smuggle out to devour in their rooms or in front of the TV, the extravagant meals we enjoy around the round table outside in summer or at the square table in the dining room in winter, everything comes from the kitchen. Of course, everything also goes back to the kitchen in the shape of leftovers and dirty dishes, so that the eternal cycle can continue. That's what the circle of life really means here in Church Street.

There are more reasons why the kitchen plays a central role in our home. It's next to the front door, with an uninterrupted view of the rickety front gate, so that you feel like an old-fashioned keeper of the city gate. From the kitchen you can observe the coming and going of friends and strangers alike.

The kitchen is where everyone converges, where we talk about nothing in particular, where we have our most vehement arguments, where my daughter throws her worst tantrums. The story of our lives in Church Street cannot possibly end anywhere else.

Look, there is my husband at the stove, cooking. Not small and dark and Mediterranean, as I've already told you, but also not big and blond and Flemish. Something in-between, I'd say, an interesting compromise between north and south, between cold and heat, between mind and body.

By the way, if you don't like garlic, then I suggest you hold your nose. Tonight we're eating la grande *aïoli*, a festive Mediterranean dish in which garlic plays the leading role. And Alain always adds a little more garlic than any recipe requires. Just in case. To ward off colds and vampires. Because there's no such thing as enough when it comes to garlic.

If you don't like loud rock music, you'll also have to plug your ears. Alain cannot cook without music. Well, neither can he shave, bath, drive his car, knock nails into a wall or carry out any other everyday activity without music. The louder the better. Anything from rock to baroque. From lieder to blues. From opera to punk. Tonight it's Lou Reed and Patti Smith, but it could equally have been Glenn Gould and Kathleen Ferrier.

If you can stand the noise and the garlic fumes, then please make yourself at home. Pull up a chair next to the wooden table, pour yourself a drink, let's see what the Frenchman is up to.

He has just crushed a dozen fat garlic cloves, while swaying his body to the beat of *Beginning of a Great Adventure*, and now he's mixing them with two egg yolks. (Fresh eggs that were laid by a friend's free-range chickens this morning.) Never mind *The Naked Chef*; meet the dancing, singing chef. There's a dirty mark on his worn blue jersey, and his dark hair is sticking up in every direction, but he couldn't care less. There's no room for vanity at the stove. He frowns with concentration as he arrives at the next very important step.

Half a litre of pure virgin olive oil (of which we have an enviable variety in this region) is poured in a thin stream into the garlicky egg yolks while he beats the mixture with the other hand. Like making mayonnaise, he explains over his shoulder. Lazy cooks like me who have never made their own mayonnaise will of course get little benefit from this instruction. The French store-bought version is good enough for me, thank you. Especially after seeing how much patience it costs my husband to achieve the perfect texture for this little sauce.

I suppose you could cheat and just add a lot of garlic to the best jar of mayonnaise you can buy – but that would really hint of bad sportsmanship. The sauce is the essence of this dish, the ingredient that gives *aïoli* its name; all the others revolve around it. If you're not prepared to put a little effort into the sauce, then you should rather serve your guests a pot of pasta.

Your guests, I say, because la grande *aïoli* is not the sort of thing you make for your ungrateful family. It entails too many different dishes on the table – and far too much washing up afterwards. But it's a winner when you have to entertain large numbers of people. The vegetables can be made ahead of time and served lukewarm or even cold. You don't have to rush around the kitchen at the eleventh hour and join the guests with sweat stains under your armpits. You can relax along with your guests. And if the hostess is relaxed, I always maintain, her guests can't help following her example.

Tonight we're entertaining our first large group of guests of The Season. Yes, believe it or not, a year has passed since I started writing this account last spring. Thomas has meanwhile turned eighteen, earned the right to vote – and exercised it for the first time in a recent interim election – and will soon embark on the French version of the matric exam. Daniel and Hugo are both twelve and at the end of their first year at *college*. And Mia's playschool class is already rehearsing the songs (with more enthusiasm than musical talent) that they'll have to sing at the end-of-year concert in June.

We could sense spring in the air – at last! – when we opened our eyes this morning. The European spring is much more clear-ly demarcated than those vague and transient few days between cold and heat in Africa. Around here spring is a specific season for which you need specific clothing that you can neither wear in the icy winter nor in the sweltering summer. And if the winter has been particularly bleak and chill, as the past one was, the spring is of course particularly welcome.

We didn't have a snowy winter this year, just an incessantly windy one. Twice we saw a white swirl of flakes against the pale sky, but each time the thin layer on the ground melted within hours. Not even enough to prevent the school bus from coming to pick up the children. Deep disappointment for Daniel. What is the point of a European winter if you don't miss even a single day of school because of snow? 'We could just as well have been in Africa!' he exclaimed miserably. Indeed.

We may not have had any snow but the nagging wind guaranteed that we were shivering with cold. One recent night, our neighbours' aged shepherd froze to death just outside the village. He'd been trying to rescue a sheep from a ditch, fell into the ditch himself and froze to death within hours. Our resident meteorologist and historian says that he hasn't experienced such an unusually windy, snowless winter since childhood. Unusual, says Jean-Pierre while absentmindedly stroking his moustache, but no cause for concern. Some years the weather is just strange. That's the way it's always been around here, since his great-great-grandfather's day, and that's the way it always will be. *C'est comme ça.*

All I know is that for several weeks I've been looking forward to spring with more than usual impatience. That's the reason I jumped out of bed this morning (usually I stagger from between the sheets like the living dead) and flung open the bedroom windows to admire the first yellow tulips in the garden below. For a moment I considered doing something completely daft to celebrate the arrival of spring. Like jogging around the block. Just for a moment. Then the strange urge passed and I once again became my usual lazy self and waited for my husband to bring me coffee.

Now it is several hours later and there is no time left to be lazy. Everyone in the house has to pitch in, even if the children do so moaning and groaning. Daniel and Hugo are laying the square dining table with a Provençal tablecloth (blue and yellow, with a motif of olives and sunflowers, what else?), under strict maternal supervision because otherwise they'll place the knives and forks the wrong way round and forget the napkins. Thomas plays the guitar for Mia, supposedly to keep her from getting under our feet, but really just because he'd rather play the guitar than do anything else. Alain takes care of the sauce and the fish, and I am the chef's assistant who has to lend a hand with all the other dishes.

Aïoli is one of those versatile dishes that you can make up as you go along. In Provence the only really indispensable ingredients are the garlic mayonnaise and the *morue salée* – salted cod, which according to the epicure Auguste Escoffier should preferably come from the cold seas around Iceland. But you know, these days you take what you can get. Then you soak the fish for at least twelve hours in water that must be replaced regularly to get rid of the salt. It is such a time-consuming process that I once asked in all innocence if one couldn't just buy fresh cod instead.

I mean, what's the point of a salted fish that has to be desalted with so much fuss?

Oh dear. The consternation on Madame Voisine's face instantly told me that I'd made yet another *faux pas*. After all I should know better by now. For the French, no fuss is too great when it comes to making food or making love.

For la grande *aïoli* you use desalted salted fish, Madame Voisine assures me. Anything else would be sacrilege.

Now if you want to spoil your friends with *aïoli* in South Africa and you can't lay your hands on a piece of *morue*, then I suppose you could use fresh fish. Something like hake, perhaps, something with a neutral, undistinctive taste. But don't tell Madame Voisine (or even my husband) I said so.

Here in Church Street we do things properly. Our fillets of *morue* have been soaking since last night. Alain has replaced the water many times and now the fish is finally ready to be gently poached. In the meantime, I have boiled some eggs and a variety of vegetables. Young potatoes *en robe de chambre*, in their dressing gowns, as the poetic French say when referring to something as prosaic as potatoes cooked in their skins. The tiny carrots and slim green beans should still be a little crunchy, and the little artichokes and baby marrows should also not be cooked to a pulp. You can add beetroot and broccoli, or even cauliflower and fresh peas, any vegetable, really, that doesn't lose its flavour when it is simply boiled in water. Not eggplant or mushrooms or anything that should rather be baked or fried. Tonight we do without the beetroot – there'll be more than enough to eat – and we're serving the broccoli raw. With a few firm tomatoes cut into wedges. Raw, of course.

Daniel and Hugo, still grumbling, will soon help me arrange everything on large platters. The idea is to play the various textures and colours off one against the other. The white flakiness of the fish and the firm yellow hearts of the egg halves. The dull green shine of the cooked artichokes and the crisp deep green of the raw broccoli. The carrots' bright orange and the tomatoes' bright red. A rainbow on the table, as it were, with the pale-yellow garlic sauce like the legendary pot of gold at one end of its curve.

Guests are served a generous spoonful of sauce and help themselves to the rest of the food. You're really supposed to drag every bite through the sauce before bringing it anywhere near your mouth, but you can also get away with dipping something briefly into the sauce every now and then. We usually have a jar or ordinary, innocuous mayonnaise on the table for the children and those rare souls who can't handle so much garlic in one go.

But don't tell Madame Voisine. I can already see those thin pencil lines on her forehead shape themselves into arches: *aïoli* without garlic? *Quelle horreur!* It'd be like lemon tart without lemons!

With such an elaborate main course we don't bother with a time-consuming starter. Nor with a complicated dessert. Three or four good cheeses will usually do – one made from cow's milk, one from goat's milk and one from sheep's milk. Along with enough fresh bread – a long one made with white flour and a round one made with whole-wheat – for those who may still have a little gap to fill. But we can't get away without appetisers. Tradition is tradition, after all.

Just as a top athlete wouldn't dream of competing without warming up his muscles, a French eater won't venture upon a meal without first warming up his taste buds. This is where *l'apéritif* comes in – little bites to amuse the mouth while the first drink of the evening is served.

And this is why, before we display the *aïoli*, I am dishing a variety of olives into a bowl. (Alain is tending his desalted salted fish like a tender baby. Lou Reed is singing, *You need a busload of faith to get by*.) And I am marvelling at the olives.

I not only live in the best truffle region in France, I also live in the best olive region. How lucky can one woman be? The famous silver orchards and old-fashioned olive-oil mills of Nyons are barely twenty minutes from our front door. And since I cannot afford to spoil my guests with truffles, I like to overwhelm them with olives. My favourite appetiser is a table spread with them.

The place of honour goes to the whole olives that you can buy at any morning market: green ones and black ones, pickled with chilli, flavoured with fennel, sprinkled with basil, pitted and stuffed with slivers of red pepper. The choice never ceases to astound me. With the olives I serve slices of French bread that have been drizzled with olive oil and quickly grilled in the oven. They're best hot out of the oven, but even cold our boys can't resist them. It's also a practical way of getting rid of yesterday's leftover bread. As you know, a *baguette* is something that must be eaten straight away, or it becomes as hard as a stick. (In fact, the French word means a staff or a chopstick.) By late afternoon there's always a leftover piece of *baguette* no one wants to touch. That's when I get out the olive oil and turn on the oven.

On our table there'll also be a basket of fresh bread, and a bowl of the best olive oil I can afford, so that guests can drizzle a little oil over their own piece of bread. Or dunk the bread in the oil – why not? You seldom see butter on tables around here. Bread is eaten dry, or drizzled with olive oil. Apparently it is one of the reasons Mediterranean people live so long, even though they smoke and drink far too much.

I sometimes buy a special bread studded with bits of olives from the local baker. And now and then a bowl of *tapenade*, a fragrant pâté made from black or green olives. And there is usually a plump dried sausage stuffed with nuts, just in case someone happens to be allergic to olives. And to prevent the carnivores among us from getting withdrawal symptoms.

By now Daniel and Hugo will have lit the candles in the dining room. Alain has just taken the *morue* from the oven and, because applause is due, Thomas has briefly put down his guitar. Like most male chefs, my husband cannot cook without applause.

Mia grabs the chance to stuff a few olives into her mouth while everyone's attention is on the fish. If you're born here, you start sucking on olives as soon as you have teeth. Lou Reed is singing, *You better hold on – something's happening here*. And I'm keeping an eye on the garden gate because our first guests will arrive at any moment.

Have you finished your drink? Would you like to join us for dinner? When we make *aïoli*, there's always enough for an extra plate. Help yourself to some olives in the meantime, before my daughter finishes the lot. By now you should feel quite at home here among us. After all, it's been a year since you first tasted *pastis* on the verandah of our local bar.

Bon appétit.

France
April 2004